SEVEN PERSONAL WAYS FOR DEVELOPING YOUR POTENTIAL

PERSONAL GROWTH IS PERSONAL

ABRAM GOMEZ

WHAT PEOPLE ARE SAYING ABOUT *PERSONAL GROWTH IS PERSONAL*

Have you ever felt like you had more within you but just didn't know how to get it out? In *Personal Growth is Personal*, Abram Gomez provides a powerful blueprint to help you unlock the potential that resides within you. Abram will challenge you to think beyond your current place in life and look towards a brighter future!

—Tamara Lowe
Founder and CEO at Kingdom Builders Academy
New York Times Best Selling Author
"America's #1 Christian Business Coach"

Abram offers the reader time-proven insights that are universal in their application, ideal for anyone seeking to GROW. It also happens to be a great read, sure to be a great gift for colleagues, friends, and your loved ones!

—Daniel Garza
Founder and President of The Libre Initiative

Personal Growth Is Personal is more than a book; it's a menu of what is not only possible but attainable. In its pages, you will find the framework of the practical tools you need to begin the process of becoming the person you always knew you could be. In a world filled with self-help literature, this book stands out as a genuine and compassionate companion on the road to personal transformation. I wholeheartedly recommend it to anyone ready to embark on a journey of self-discovery and growth!

—Pastor Jaime Loya
Senior Pastor of Cross Church, one of America's
largest bilingual multisite churches

Copyright © 2024 by Abram Gomez

Published by Arrows and Stones

All rights reserved. No portion of this book may be reproduced, stored in a retrieval system, or transmitted in any form or by any means—electronic, mechanical, photocopy, recording, scanning, or other—except for brief quotations in critical reviews or articles, without prior written permission of the author.

Scripture quotations marked KJV are taken from the King James Version of the Bible. Public domain. | Scripture quotations marked MSG are taken from THE MESSAGE, copyright © 1993, 1994, 1995, 1996, 2000, 2001, 2002 by Eugene H. Peterson. Used by permission of NavPress. All rights reserved. Represented by Tyndale House Publishers, Inc. | Scripture quotations marked NIV are taken from the Holy Bible, New International Version®, NIV®. Copyright © 1973, 1978, 1984, 2011 by Biblica, Inc.™ Used by permission of Zondervan. All rights reserved worldwide. www.zondervan.com. The "NIV" and "New International Version" are trademarks registered in the United States Patent and Trademark Office by Biblica, Inc.™ | Scripture quotations marked NKJV are taken from the New King James Version®. Copyright © 1982 by Thomas Nelson. Used by permission. All rights reserved.

For foreign and subsidiary rights, contact the author.

Cover design by Sara Young
Cover photo by: Jeanette G. Zapata Photography

ISBN: 978-1-960678-81-2   1 2 3 4 5 6 7 8 9 10

Printed in the United States of America

I want to dedicate this book to my parents who raised me as their own—Emmett and Mary Gomez. They are no longer in this world, yet their life continues to impact mine and our family's. Dad and Mom: this is for you because you were the first to believe in me. You always said I was set apart.

CONTENTS

CHAPTER 1. **Personal Story** 9

CHAPTER 2. **Personal Awareness** 23

CHAPTER 3. **Personal Mindset** 39

CHAPTER 4. **Personal Communication** 57

CHAPTER 5. **Personal Environment** 69

CHAPTER 6. **Personal Relationships** 83

CHAPTER 7. **Personal Habits** 97

CHAPTER 8. **Personal Growth** 109

CHAPTER 9. **Die Empty** 119

Resources 131

CHAPTER 1

PERSONAL STORY

*"I never knew how much hard work
it would take to be effective."*
—John Maxwell

PERSONAL STORY

HELLO. MY NAME IS ABRAM GOMEZ.

Before we dive together into this book, let me just say thank you. Thank you for taking the time to get a copy of my book and taking time out of your life and schedule to actually read it. If you are reading this, something connected you to it. I would like to think it was divine. Or spiritual providence. Or maybe you just liked the cover. Whatever the case, you have it and here we are.

I wrote this book for two reasons: because I felt from the Lord to do so and because I wanted to write a book for people who have always felt they are on the outside looking in. Trust me—I know exactly what that feels like. That's a feeling, if not confronted or understood, that tends to linger in your mind and heart. And if you are like most people, you may not even know where to look, how to start, where to begin, or even what to do about it. All you know is that you have more potential than your life actually shows. I like to say in the words of musical artist John Mayer: "I'm bigger than my body gives me credit for."[1] I really don't know why he wrote that song, but for me, I have often felt bigger than life gave me credit for. Perhaps that's you. If so, you are not alone. Throughout your reading, you are going to get the teacher in me,

---

[1] John Mayer, vocalist, "Bigger Than My Body," by John Mayer, August 11, 2003, track 2 on *Heavier Things*, Aware and Columbia Records.

PERSONAL GROWTH IS PERSONAL

the leader in me, and the human in me. You'll gain insight, you'll be provided direction, and you'll see that you don't have to be perfect or have it all figured out to begin.

> **I like to think that potential is the breath of God in our lives.**

Dr. Myles Munroe once said that potential is "unused success."[2] To me, this is such a profound statement and here is why: it communicates that I have more success, more victory, more progress, and more traction in me. So do you. Everything you need to accomplish your future is already within you. You don't release destiny; you discover it. You don't run to your future; you release it. Say that out loud: "I will release my future." I like to think that potential is the breath of God in our lives. Genesis 2:7 (NKJV) states, "And the Lord God formed man of the dust of the ground, and breathed into his nostrils the breath of life; and man became a living being." The breath of life is flowing in you in this very minute and in this very hour. And as long as you have the breath of life, you have potential. Life gives birth to life. And if we aren't aware of this fact, we could squander or sit on all that God has given to us. We have potential until the day we die.

Think with me for a moment: you still have unused success. But the question must be asked: what do you plan to do about it? I was in this same predicament in 2011 when I came across a line

---
2 Myles Munroe, *Understanding Your Potential* (Shippensburg PA: Destiny Image Publishers, 1992) 21.

PERSONAL STORY

in a book by John Maxwell, *The 15 Invaluable Laws of Growth*, that said the following on the first page of the first chapter: "Do you have a plan for your personal growth?"[3]

That was it. That's all it took, and my life was changed. Again.

As I sat in my office in that moment pondering if I had what it took to be in the current position I was in at a large and growing church, I picked up this book by John Maxwell that I really didn't remember where I'd purchased it. Or even when I had bought the book. I'd like to think that I knew what I was doing when I bought it, but the reality is I think I just stumbled upon it.

Have you ever bought a book that you wanted to read and just never got around to doing that? Let me state for the record—I hope this book isn't one of those books for you. ☺ It was that moment on a warm afternoon that I had an epiphany.

You see—I had this feeling that I had not experienced in a long time. It was a feeling that I was way in over my head. I had just been promoted to executive pastor of one of the fastest-growing bilingual churches in America. I had a pretty good season of being a youth pastor, and I knew that the Lord opened the door for me to keep fulfilling the ministry He placed on my life. However, I really didn't have a clue about how to be an effective executive pastor—or what they really did for that matter. It was kind of a new developing role in our church organization due to the growth. All I knew was that it came with a more prestigious title and more responsibility within the organization, and there I sat feeling something that maybe you can relate to—I felt I

---

[3] John C. Maxwell, *The 15 Invaluable Laws of Growth: Live Them and Reach Your Potential* (New York, NY: Center Street, 2012) 1.

had been promoted beyond my potential. I also didn't know how to get better.

For the record, potential is one of my favorite words in our vocabulary, and I will share more about that later, but for that particular moment in my personal history, I felt that my potential was maxed out like a credit card, and I didn't have any way to increase it. I hadn't yet developed the perspective that my potential was limitless.

When I opened up the book and read that line, "Do you have a plan for your personal growth?" it hit me. I remember placing the book down, and I just stared into space as if something clicked on the inside. I put two and two together. *That's it!* I thought. That's why I felt the way that I had felt. That's why I felt stuck in a season. That's why I didn't feel I was making any progress. It was as if I was waiting for something or someone to come knock on my door, send me an email, or something and tell me that I was going to get better supernaturally. But, none of that happened. I was waiting for others when the real person I was waiting for was me.

I was waiting for me to wake up.

I was waiting for me to believe.

I was waiting for me to do something about it.

I was waiting for me to grow.

What if I told you that rather than needing others to believe in you, you need you to believe in yourself more? What good is it if the whole world believes in you, and you don't even believe in you?

THE START OF SOMETHING SPECIAL

After I came out of that moment, I eagerly read the entire first chapter of the book that day. And I couldn't stop. The way he

PERSONAL STORY

put the book together made me feel like anyone could grow and that growth wasn't for the wealthy, the elite, or "them," but it was for anyone willing to develop themselves. He made it seem possible that someone like me could grow into someone better. As I read the words and insight, I felt as if something within me was opening up. I would liken it to a pipe being unclogged as my mind began to flow with new thoughts and endless possibilities. I read all of it within a month highlighting phrases that stood out to me. I reread some chapters just to make sure I understood it correctly. And, by the end of it, I walked away with a plan. Not just any type of plan, but a growth plan.

I hadn't put together a growth plan EVER. I went to high school and graduated. I even went to college and graduated. But that was different . . . this was different. Lots of people never read or personally develop after any type of schooling. We just assume we are going to keep growing and getting better, but that's not always the case. Life happens, and for many of us, we get stuck and complacent, or we just don't have the time. We continually replay a mental loop of our lives, or we tend to believe the best of us is behind us. Many people know there is more, but things get in the way of their growth. Before we know it, we are caught in a never-ending cycle of our week-to-week routine. Months will pass. Years will pass. Hope fades. Regret tries to set in. All because we know we have more, but we just haven't broken through. Many of us eventually resign and settle for what we think: *This is it for me.* With a renewed sense of optimism in my heart, I decided to stop having pity for myself. I would try something I had not done, and that was to follow the advice of John Maxwell and devise a plan to grow.

PERSONAL GROWTH IS PERSONAL

> **Growth doesn't just happen, you know. You can grow either by the school of hard knocks, or you can grow by the school of intentionality.**

Growth doesn't just happen, you know. You can grow either by the school of hard knocks, or you can grow by the school of intentionality.

In my plan to grow, I wrote three things that I would do to grow for the following year. Now, for the record, the book didn't tell me to choose three things. It told me a lot of things, but sometimes, we can feel so overwhelmed by the information and data we paralyze ourselves and stop even before we get started. I made a decision to do three things because I felt they were attainable and doable. I selected items on my growth plan that were within my reach. At the end of the day, I just wanted to get started, and from what I read, any progress is good progress. My first growth plan looked like this:

1) Read twenty-four books for the year—two a month.
2) Listen to one podcast a week.
3) Meet with a new person every week.

First, I began to immediately put together the list of books that I wanted to read, which, to be quite honest, was not very long to begin with. I wrote down a lot of books by John Maxwell, as well as any other Christian leader I could think of during that season. I did some research on good books to read and selected some from that list as well.

PERSONAL STORY

Why are books so important to read? Insight. Remember, you are limited in your experience and what you know. By reading about topics and things from others, we can learn and gain knowledge. Maybe you don't have any mentors right now in your life, but did you know that there are plenty of "mentors" waiting on you at your local bookstore? You may not be able to sit down and have lunch with someone who really inspires you or someone that you admire, but you can engage with their way of thinking through their writings. You can meet people who have left this life by reading the works they left behind.

Secondly, I searched for good, insightful podcasts. Listening to new podcasts was part of my growth plan because I not only wanted to read about things from others, but I wanted to hear about things from others. Sometimes, as a person is speaking, you catch things by their tone and cadence that you cannot catch while reading. Some things are taught, while others things are caught. During that time, podcasting was beginning to take off, and I felt it was a great tool for learning. Also, podcasts are shorter and a bit more accessible, as most are absolutely free.

Lastly, I was very methodical in meeting with a new person every week. I was part of a large Christian community, but I found that many of us have this particular habit of comfort. We tend to go to lunch with the same people—all the time. We tend to hang out with the same people—all the time. The older we get, the more set in our ways we become. Plus, I remember reading in Dr. Henry Cloud's book *Integrity: The Courage to Meet the Demands of Reality* that if we stay around the same people all the time, we may not have any new perspectives or thoughts come

PERSONAL GROWTH IS PERSONAL

into our mind to challenge our way of thinking.[4] I felt that by meeting with new people on a weekly basis, I could learn, listen, and grow. All I did was reach out to people from my church and around my community and ask them if they wanted to do lunch. This included people that I hardly knew or just wanted to connect with and hear their story. This was a game changer as it taught me how to network and learn about others.

When 2012 rolled around, I was ready. I had my growth plan. I had enthusiasm, and I went for it. Let me tell you, by the end of that year, it happened. I grew. And, I didn't feel like I just grew . . . I felt like I had grown by leaps and bounds. There are some verses in the Bible that, if you aren't familiar with them, it's okay. I just think it's important for me to bring them up for your recognition and remembrance:

- 1 Samuel 3:19 (NKJV): "So Samuel grew, and the LORD was with him and let none of his words fall to the ground."
- Luke 2:52 (NIV): "And Jesus grew in wisdom and stature, and in favor with God and man."

Do you see it? They *grew*—and the Lord was with them. Both Samuel and Jesus had specific roles to play in their lives that required their personal and spiritual growth. Samuel served his generation by developing his gift through his growth. Jesus served (and is still serving) all of us by His unwavering commitment to complete the Father's assignment. Each filled their role.

---

4   Henry Cloud, *Integrity: The Courage to Meet the Demands of Reality* (New York, NY: Harper, 2009).

PERSONAL STORY

> **You may not know this because maybe no one has told you, but there are people out there depending on your growth.**

You have a role to play in this life to fulfill your purpose and influence others: your children, your clients, and your audience. You may not know this because maybe no one has told you, but there are people out there depending on your growth. Craig Groeschel, senior pastor of Life.Church, says, "Everyone wins when the leader gets better."[5]

Here is the best news. Like Samuel and Jesus, YOU CAN GROW TOO!

YOUR GROWTH IS THE GIFT THAT KEEPS ON GIVING

Since that year, I have framed a phrase that I constantly use when spreading the importance of personal growth: your growth is the gift that keeps on giving. When you continually grow and invest in yourself, everything around you begins to change. Your world seems to grow larger and larger. Your heart expands. Your vision increases. And once you have captured something such as an idea or a principle, it's yours forever. You cannot unknow it. Your growth will keep giving to your life well beyond when a book,

---

5 Craig Groeschel, Twitter post, August 6, 2020, 9:45 a.m., https://twitter.com/craiggroeschel/status/1291369887663882240?lang=en.

PERSONAL GROWTH IS PERSONAL

lecture, or seminar ends. Your growth could potentially bring you a promotion, a new job, or the right people.

This book was written with a main focus to help you grow but more importantly, to let you know that you can indeed experience growth in your life. Growth begins when we become aware of our need for it as well as our potential for it. In the church world, we overemphasize things like anointing—valuable and necessary in its own right—and we underemphasize things like personal awareness.

At the end of 2012, I felt more confident in who I was. I had new doors of opportunity open for my life that had been closed prior. But why did this all happen? I was always "anointed," but I wasn't always aware. When I became more aware of where I was, who I was, and what I needed to do, the anointing became clearer over and through my life.

For many years, I was living life below my potential. I always knew there was something deeper, but I didn't know how to unleash it or how to even open the lock. Once I discovered my passion for learning and growth, though, something changed. I would never be the same again. Moreover, I knew that I had stumbled upon a helpful message not just for me but for anyone who has felt this way. Writing a book was deep within my heart, but I didn't know what theme or topic it would cover. When I decided I would write about personal growth, I immediately thought to myself, *There are plenty of books on self-help and growth. Why me?* Then I read a quote that changed my mind: "Sure, it has been said before, but not by you." That's when I knew. Others—like you—need to hear this message.

PERSONAL STORY

> **You are your greatest investment, and you are your greatest investor. No one will invest in you the way you will.**

And guess what? You also have a personal story with tests and triumphs that God can use as a testimony to bless others! Your personal story is filled with grace and mercy. Don't allow a mindset or environment to hold you back. There's more because God has made you more. You are your greatest investment, and you are your greatest investor. No one will invest in you the way you will.

Let's grow together.

PRAYER FOR YOUR PERSONAL STORY:

Father, thank You for the gift of life and my journey. I believe that You have more reserved for me and that You are guarding my portion. No enemy or person can take away what You have set apart for me. Help me to remember that my story is valuable and that You work all things together for Your good and for Your purpose over my life. I surrender all things to You in this moment, and I trust in Your guidance.
   In Jesus' name. Amen.

CHAPTER 2

PERSONAL AWARENESS

"Until you make the unconscious conscious, it will direct your life and you will call it fate."
—Often attributed to C. G. Jung

PERSONAL AWARENESS

I HAVE LEARNED THAT YOU NEVER KNOW WHEN something will be birthed in your heart and mind. Ideas come in different shapes and sizes. Burdens are placed in your life in moments you least expect. God dreams can be initiated in a season you didn't see coming. A gift can be activated in some of the lowest places in your life.

People in my world have often asked me why I like to help people grow. And the story I am about to share with you is one of the main reasons I have a passion for helping people grow and become more aware of who they are, especially in the Lord.

I grew up in church, but, like a typical church teenager, I got away from the church during my adolescence. My father stopped attending church, and I eventually followed his lead. I didn't really see much of a need for faith in my life although I kept what I had learned as a child in my heart. I lived the usual teenage life full of temptation, friends, and small-town fun. In 1999, my mother invited me to a service that the church was hosting for young people. I had visited the church at different moments throughout the year, but nothing seemed to hit my heart. The pastors were great people, but I just didn't see a connection between church and purpose. I felt I was already moving in a direction of my choosing. At that time, I was nineteen years old and attending McLennan Community College in Waco, Texas. My collegiate pursuit was nursing. When I received the invite from my mother,

PERSONAL GROWTH IS PERSONAL

I knew that the church was going to bring in a guest speaker, so I figured I would give it a shot.

Having a guest speaker usually meant hearing from someone different, and the timing of the invite couldn't be more favorable. It was a fortunate stroke of serendipity because what was about to happen would completely change my life. I was in a season of searching for deeper meaning, and going to church seemed like an intervention rather than an interruption.

Growing up in Sunday school and in a church setting, I had already heard about Jesus and even accepted Him as a younger child, but during that specific service, I encountered His presence like never before. When the preacher (who is now a great friend of mine) asked for people to come forward to respond to the message, I remember standing to my feet and going forward. This was out of character for me as I usually preferred to stay away from the front of the church where others could see me. I just didn't want to appear vulnerable or "needy."

Tears of joy, fulfillment, and love would flow from my eyes for the next forty-five minutes during that service. It was as if a faucet was turned on internally, and I was being cleansed from the inside out. I just knew my life had changed.

That same night, I went home still feeling "the presence of the Lord." I lay down in my bed, weeping. I fell asleep with tears cascading down my face. The very next day, I could literally hear the birds chirping outside my window. The sky seemed like it was such a vivid blue that I had never noticed before. Again, I just knew my life had changed.

THE DISCOVERY OF A CALLING

From that day forward, I wanted to serve the Lord with all my heart. I began to read the Word. I began to actually take time to pray and seek His face. I went to the pastors of the church and told them about my experience. I shared my testimony with others of how I encountered Jesus in a very personal way. Soon after that, I began to help out at my church by playing drums and helping out with the youth, since I was a young adult myself. My life began to have meaning, and my renewed faith gave my pain a purpose. I was in the beginning stages of transformation, but I could already sense a calling over my life. It's amazing what happens to you when you surrender. When you stop trying to force it your way. Surrender is allowing Him to do it His way.

Surrender your own thoughts about yourself.

Surrender your own plans and trust His.

Surrender your failures for His promises.

You may be thinking, *So, if I surrender, everything will work?* Well, it's definitely a start. So many of us resist and say no—to God, to growth, to opportunity, and to change. We make excuses about not having enough time, money, or bandwidth, but what if I told you that your surrender could be the key that unlocks the first door to your growth? It was in my personal surrender to the Lord and to His development that my own journey of growth began. I just gave up on doing my way.

Right around that season of change, I heard about this major youth conference happening near our area, and we decided that it would be a good idea to take our youth to it. They were going to have a major Christian band playing along with a great speaker, and we thought, *Why not?* So, when the day had arrived, we loaded up the van with our youth, with excitement brewing in the air, and we proceeded to our destination about an hour away. Once we arrived, we walked toward the building and walked in. We didn't really see anyone at the front, so we went to sit down in the huge auditorium. I remember thinking to myself that I was so grateful to be there, and I knew that the students were going to enjoy it.

Well, what happened next was a huge lesson learned for me that I will never forget. The moment I am about to describe is the genesis of why I have a passion for helping people grow and become more aware. This was a moment of misery that became an understanding of ministry and purpose for me. I have often said that your misery (what makes you miserable) can become your ministry (what you do to help serve others so that they don't experience that misery).

> **I have often said that your misery can become your ministry.**

While we were patiently waiting in the auditorium, sitting in the front row, a person came to where we were sitting and asked us why we were in there. We told them we had never been to an event like that before, and we didn't really know where to go, so we just walked in. They told us we couldn't be there and asked us to exit the room. Let me be clear—today, I understand that they were not being cold-hearted or rude. They were simply following instructions and what they knew to do. So, they pointed us in the direction of where we should go—which was a registration table. At the table, we told them we were there for the concert, but the organizers informed us that the event was for denominational churches that had already registered.

Bummer for us since we were not a part of that specific network.

Since we had neither done the prior work of registration nor were we connected to any other church from that denomination, we were not allowed to attend that evening. Honestly, our group and team were kind of clueless at that point as to what to do next. So, we kind of looked at each other and headed outside to regroup and decide what our next step would be. My leader at that time felt it was best to go ahead, leave, take the group out to eat, and make the most of the night, under the circumstances. So we did.

To be real with you, on the drive home, I felt deflated. I felt like I had failed somehow. I took it personally. I didn't like what I was feeling. I didn't blame my leader, the hosts of the conference, or even the person who asked us to go to the table—I blamed myself. Why? For simply not knowing. Sometimes, what you don't know CAN hurt you.

Have you ever had a moment where you just didn't know what you didn't know? I have. It's not always a bad thing. Sometimes, you don't know because it's new, and you are stepping out in faith. Other times, you don't know because you have never been that way before. Then there are times when you don't know because you didn't ask to know.

PERSONAL GROWTH IS PERSONAL

I know what you are thinking: *Abram, you didn't know. Don't be so hard on yourself.* You're right. We stepped out in faith to take some kids to a conference, and we didn't really know all of the information. We just wanted the students to experience something amazing. Jesus had changed my life, and I wanted others to experience the same thing.

Being informed and being aware kind of go hand in hand. Not having all the information doesn't have to prevent forward movement, but knowing you don't have all the information is called awareness. We didn't have the information for the event, and we didn't know that we didn't have all the information. Make sense? Truly, some people never grow because they don't know how to grow. They may not even know that they need to grow. They are not aware or informed. John Maxwell said that people change when four things happen:

> People change when they hurt enough, they have to. When they see enough, they're inspired to. When they learn enough that they want to, and when they receive enough that they're able to.[6]

I have always said that an informed leader is an equipped leader. In other words, when a person knows better, they have a better chance of performing better. Equipping happens when you gain the knowledge and insight you didn't have before.

It was at this moment that I told myself that if I ever became someone influential or with access to greater, I would do my

---

[6] John Maxwell, "4 Reasons to Believe People Can Change," *HarperCollins Leadership Essentials*, 26 Jan. 2021, hcleadershipessentials.com/blogs/leadership/4-reasons-to-believe-people-can-change.

best to help others—those who felt like they were on the outside looking in—actually come through the door. Again, that's why I am writing this book. To help people come into the room of their personal greatness.

In retrospect, I can now see a lot of our mistakes in that moment. First, we were simply not aware of who, what, when, and where. We also didn't ask enough questions, or at least the right questions. We assumed.

I have coached and mentored lots of leaders over the years. One of the biggest challenges that I see in people is what I saw in me years ago—a lack of personal awareness. What if the thing holding you back right now isn't that you lack the gift but that you lack the awareness that you even have the gift?

KNOW THYSELF

What good is a gift if you don't know you have it?

One common theme of great leaders or people who make a huge impact in the kingdom is that they know who they are. Confusion rarely sits in the seat of greatness. We often relate to people who don't know who they are, but we admire people who know who they are.

In the Bible, one of the most iconic figures is the apostle Paul. Paul wrote two-thirds of the New Testament, and even he didn't shy away from who he was.

Take a look at how he opened some of his letters:

- Romans 1:1 (NKJV): "Paul, a bondservant of Jesus Christ, called to be an apostle, separated to the gospel of God. . . ."

PERSONAL GROWTH IS PERSONAL

- 1 Corinthians 1:1 (NKJV): "Paul, called to be an apostle of Jesus Christ through the will of God, and Sosthenes our brother...."
- Ephesians 1:1 (NKJV): "Paul, an apostle of Jesus Christ by the will of God...."

On different occasions and to different audiences, in his opening salutation, Paul identified who he was to his readers. His own pen records terms like "called" and "by the will of God" to display his confidence in who he was.

Do you know who you are?

If you answer no, don't worry. I didn't either, but when I discovered who I was—there was no turning back. I am believing that this is the moment and season that you will discover who you are in the Lord and begin the journey of becoming who He has called you to be in your lifetime.

In the time of Instagram and TikTok, we have a great opportunity to learn about others by what they share, post, and talk about. These are really great tools! But, as you know, they're also great time wasters. If not guarded and if we don't use precaution, we can spend HOURS observing others, living vicariously through their lives, and easily forget all about our own lives.

> **We live in a time where we learn a great amount about others, but we don't learn about ourselves.**

PERSONAL AWARENESS

I think that's where the problem lies. We live in a time where we learn a great amount about others, but we don't learn about ourselves. We use all of this time and energy to know their story, but we don't exert that same kind of focus and energy to learn about our story. Personal awareness is a necessary component of your growth. It's hard to develop yourself if you don't know yourself. Back in 1999, I didn't know who I was . . . yet. In 2011, I took another deep dive in becoming aware. This is a continual journey.

So, why is personal awareness so important? Let me share with you three reasons why this is crucial:

1) *Personal awareness is your first step toward personal growth and development.*

    Before you can impact others, before you can lead others, before you can help others—you need to be impacted, you need to be led, and you need to be helped. Not in that order, but you get the idea. It must first happen within us before it can happen through us. Moses, in the book of Exodus, was delivered before he became a deliverer.

    Everything starts with me and in me. Here is a simple equation: in me (+) through me (=) around me

2) *Personal awareness is about discovering who you are so you can develop what you have.*

    The reality is that it is difficult to develop what you have not discovered. One of my favorite sayings is found in Proverbs 25:2 (NIV): "It is the glory of God to conceal a matter; to search out a matter is the glory of kings." Before you were born, the Lord prepackaged you with everything you would need to complete and fulfill your purpose. Many times, people live their lives without ever discovering their why, their gifts, and their calling.

When you become aware, you become alive.

3) *Your purpose and passion are often interconnected.*

Your passion is inward. Your purpose is outward. Your passion is what happens in you. Your purpose is what happens through you.

Now, before you let this information overwhelm you—pause. Take a moment to reflect. Remember, God created you and knows everything about you. He isn't confused about you, and His desire is not for you to go your whole life and not know Him or who He created you to be.

Ready? Let's continue.

MAKE IT PERSONAL

Remember that story I shared with you in chapter 1 about being in my office and writing out my goals? Well, another thing I did in that season was rediscover myself.

To do that, here is what I did.

First, I spent some time with the Lord in the privacy of my own thoughts and during my week. I know this may sound like a spiritual cliche, but it's not. Private time with God can lead to blissful moments publicly. There are answers that you are looking for that are found only in silence. Socrates once said, "Beware the barrenness of a busy life." It could be work, projects, ministry, school, or you name it. If we are mired in frivolous activity, distractions, or anything that is keeping us away from time with Him, it's time to rethink priorities. I would encourage you to take

PERSONAL AWARENESS

some time this week to spend in meaningful prayer. Quieting the soul is necessary to hear His still small voice.

Secondly, I did gift tests—all kinds of gift tests.

Spiritual gift tests. Personality tests. Strengths Finder. I was determined to investigate how I was wired. I even took a DISC test. I figured it was time to get serious about me. And you can too! That's the great news. You can find free tests online and look for books on gifts.

Let me remind you—you cannot develop what you have not discovered. When I began to take different types of tests, I began to discover what I already kind of knew. It confirmed for me how I was gifted. For you, it may be a revelation. Or maybe you kind of know, but you just need an extra push of confidence. Find the time to take tests. Discover or rediscover your treasure within.

Thirdly, I asked close friends and associates to describe me in 3-5 words. Why did I do this? I wanted to see if there was any correlation between what I perceived to be my gifts and grace and how others viewed me.

Words that came back to me were leadership, coach, student, encouraging, teacher. When I received those words that were common among my peers and circle, they gave me the fuel I needed to proceed with my pursuit of who I was. Today, I coach leaders, I teach others, and I motivate with my content. What I always knew was in me has made its way through me.

> **What I always knew was in me has made its way through me.**

PERSONAL GROWTH IS PERSONAL

Ask people around you to describe you and what they feel you bring to the table. Look for common threads. Now, if someone comes back with words and gifts that you didn't realize you possess, ask them why they thought that about you. Dig a bit. Maybe they see something about you that you don't see about yourself just yet.

Are you willing to invest in yourself?

Let me close this chapter by saying this—becoming aware of who you are isn't going to happen overnight. It will occur through moments, conversations, setbacks, failures, successes, mentorship, and much more. It is a journey. Personal growth is a journey.

Jesus told His disciples in Matthew 4:19 (NKJV), "Follow Me, and I will make you fishers of men."

Think about it for a minute. Follow me, and I will make you. The making is in the following. The making is in the movement. Stagnation doesn't make anything. Moving in the right direction does.

What's holding you back?

Don't be afraid of what you might find hidden. Be more afraid of missing out on what could have been.

PRAYER FOR YOUR PERSONAL AWARENESS:

Father, thank You for knowing me the way that You do. Your Word declares in Psalm 139:1-3 (NKJV) that "You have searched me and known me. You know my sitting down and my rising up; You understand my thought afar off. You comprehend my path and my lying down, and are acquainted with all my ways." Help me to know myself and all that You have placed within me. May today be the beginning of a greater awareness of You and who You have created me to be.

In Jesus' name. Amen.

CHAPTER 3

PERSONAL MINDSET

"Whether you think you can or you think you can't, you're right."
—Henry Ford

PERSONAL MINDSET

THERE IS A PROVERB THAT HAS ALWAYS STOOD out to me: "For as he thinketh in his heart, so *is* he" (Proverbs 23:7, KJV). How we think inwardly affects how we live outwardly. Process that for a moment. Your life represents what is taking place within you. And, your life tends to move in the direction of your strongest thoughts.

At this stage in my life, I understand this principle to be accurate. But years ago, that wasn't the case. I don't have the kind of story that says I grew up struggling with drugs or alcohol because I didn't. I had family members that did. Friends around me did. I was presented with opportunities to experiment, but I was just never interested. Drugs and alcohol didn't appeal to me. I didn't need to break an addiction to those kinds of things. But you know one of the things I struggled with privately that held me bound for years?

Strong insecurities about myself.

Maybe you are thinking, *That's harmless.* The reality is that it's not. Low self-esteem or thinking that you are inferior can be detrimental to you, your potential, and your future. It will make you think you are underserving or unworthy. It will whisper in your ear that you aren't enough. Have you ever thought that about yourself? That you fall short of other people's expectations, including your own? That what you have isn't what they want or need? How you talk to others should be with respect, and how

PERSONAL GROWTH IS PERSONAL

you talk to yourself should be with value. It's hard to value what you don't believe in—including yourself. *You* will limit *you*.

> **It's hard to consistently perform in a manner that is inconsistent with the way you see yourself.**

And trust me, when it came to inferiority thinking, I had it. John Maxwell says, "People are never able to outperform their self-image."[7] You will never go beyond your mindset. You will usually perform at the level that reflects your perception of yourself. It's hard to consistently perform in a manner that is inconsistent with the way you see yourself.

Let me put it this way—there is a reason why you didn't shoot your shot.

I saw myself as inferior because of my family background. I wasn't raised by my biological parents like the other kids. We didn't really have great financial status, and I felt like we were behind everyone else. There were things about my physical appearance that I didn't like, such as my size and my smile. Throughout the years of my childhood and adolescence, I just kind of let things pile up inwardly until they became a blinder of how to accurately see myself. I felt like I didn't deserve certain people in my life. I felt like I didn't belong at the table. I wasn't

---
7 John C. Maxwell, *The 15 Invaluable Laws of Growth*, 40

PERSONAL MINDSET

good enough, or so I thought. To me, it was better not to try so I wouldn't be disappointed.

Have you ever felt that way? If you have, join the club. I'm pretty sure I could have run for president of that club.

I was drowning in a mindset flooded with negative thinking. When I encountered Christ at nineteen, as I have previously mentioned, I needed to be set free from my own thoughts. God needed to go into my mind and heart and rewire all of my neurological pathways. Ways of thinking were so ingrained in my mind that I didn't realize I was on cruise control for underperformance and under-living.

There's this story in the Bible found in the book of Numbers where Moses, the leader of Israel, commands twelve spies to go into the Promised Land to spy it out and bring back a report. The spies proceed to do as Moses instructs them, and to their surprise, it truly is a promise-filled land with houses, plenty of good fruit, and prosperous terrain.

When they came back to Moses to give him an update, they shared all that they had seen. However, ten of the twelve spies shared negatively:

But the men who had gone up with him said, "We can't attack those people; they are stronger than we are." And they spread among the Israelites a bad report about the land they had explored. They said, "The land we explored devours those living in it. All the people we saw there are of great size. We saw the Nephilim there (the descendants of Anak come from the Nephilim). We seemed like

PERSONAL GROWTH IS PERSONAL

grasshoppers in our own eyes, and we looked the same to them." —Numbers 13:31-33 (NIV)

Pay attention to their language. The words that proceed from our mouths are words that have lived in our hearts and minds. I have a question for you—would you punch yourself in a fight? Of course, you wouldn't. Yet, many of us knock ourselves down by our own words.

No one had told them they were grasshoppers. They told themselves.

Eventually, out of that bunch of spies, only two would go on to experience the Promised Land while the others were forgotten about. The two were named Joshua and Caleb. And why were they able to succeed and experience realized promises? Because they refused to think the way the other ten did.

What if I told you that the reason "they" may be succeeding in life isn't because they are more talented or more gifted than you—what if it is because they simply believe differently than you?

Belief equals behavior.

> **Belief equals behavior.**

CHANGE YOUR MIND—CHANGE YOUR LIFE

This is how I define mindset: it is the framework by which you view yourself, others, and the world. We all have a mindset by which we operate. It has been shaped by several things and continues to be shaped by the following:

Past and Current Experiences

These are what you have been through and are going through. James Allen, author of *As a Man Thinketh*, says that a person is limited only by the thoughts that he chooses.[8] I would dare say that a lot of people are incarcerated not by the felonies that they have committed, but by the thoughts that have entrapped them. The keys to freedom are not hanging in the pocket of a deputy; they are buried in the inner chambers of their mind. And all we need is a light to shine through the mental bars to show us that we have had them this entire time.

We are products of our past, but we don't have to be prisoners of them. Even though your past can affect your way of thinking, it doesn't have to be a death sentence. The good news is that you can change if you so desire. Maybe you didn't finish school, and you feel like it's too late for you. Actually, it's not. You don't need a degree to be wise.

Level of Education

When I say education, I mean both formal and informal. Again, people do better when they know better. Remember the scarecrow in the *Wizard of Oz*?[9] If you don't, let me refresh your memory. Dorothy, Kansas, Toto, Scarecrow, Tin Man, and Cowardly Lion. Warner Brothers Entertainment Wiki describes him like this:

---

8   James Allen, *As a Man Thinketh: A Guide to Unlocking the Power of Your Mind* (London, England: Thinking Ink, 2011).
9   Victor Fleming, *The Wizard of Oz* (August 25, 1939; Beverly Hills: Metro-Goldwyn-Mayer).

PERSONAL GROWTH IS PERSONAL

He is kind, friendly, helpful, clumsy, considerate, and caring. Though he is a scarecrow, he is disappointed that he cannot scare a single crow from the cornfield he lives and hates the mockery he receives. As a result of the mockery he receives, the Scarecrow feels insecure about himself and finds himself to not be the brightest creature in Oz due to being made out of straw. This causes him to desire to have a brain so he can be smart and intellectual.[10]

He is known for his melody, "If I Only Had a Brain."[11]
Here's another equation for you:

brain = mindset

Scarecrow joins Dorothy (reminder: your friends can help you or hinder you) on her journey to see the wonderful Wizard of Oz. When they get there, the Wizard says, "Everyone and all living creatures have a brain and from his homeland are seeds for great learning."[12] He then gives Scarecrow a diploma. From that point on, Scarecrow is awakened to his genius.

Let me be a voice in your story right now—we have all been given a beautiful mind, and within you are seeds of greatness. Behind all of it is your inner genius.

Circle of Friends and Family

Those closest to you influence you more than you realize. The influence your friends and family have on you is legitimate and

---

10 Contributors, "Scarecrow," *Warner Bros. Entertainment Wiki*, warnerbros.fandom.com/wiki/Scarecrow.
11 Ray Bolger, vocalist, "If I Only Had a Brain," by Harold Arlen, August 25, 1939; Beverly Hills: Metro-Goldwyn-Mayer.
12 Contributors, "Scarecrow," *Warner Bros. Entertainment Wiki*, warnerbros.fandom.com/wiki/Scarecrow.

should definitely be taken both with encouragement and caution. I say this because some people will be for you and refuel you. However, others can quench the dreams and desires that have been placed in your heart. Some of my greatest allies have been people. Some of my greatest obstacles have been people. Learning to distinguish and discern the difference is key.

Be aware—your personal growth will be an indicator as well as a separator. It will show you who is moving in the same direction as you, but it will also reveal who would prefer to stay where they are. Growth separates. Pay attention to who you are around when you feel the most edified and confident. Also, notice who you are around when you feel the most insecure. Maybe they challenge you. Maybe they aren't for you. Discern and determine. I will discuss personal relationships more in a later chapter.

Mentors and Leaders

Your mentors and leaders pass on what they know to you. I once heard a definition of mentoring, and it says that mentoring is wisdom without the wounds. Mentors and leaders are gifts to your life that can help expose you to different mindsets and ways of thinking. Oftentimes, we try to do it all by ourselves and figure it out on our own. Sure, maybe you have had some success by doing it this way, especially if you are a self-starter. But, the wisdom and insight that others further down the road can offer you are priceless. Personally, I have gone to new levels in different areas of my life because of coaches, mentors, and leaders.

When you invest in a mentor or leader, you are really investing in yourself.

PERSONAL GROWTH IS PERSONAL

> **When you invest in a mentor or leader, you are really investing in yourself.**

Location and Culture

Don't underestimate how your surroundings impact your thinking. Some of the biggest decisions we make in life are whom we decide to do life with, what we will do with our talents and gifts, how we will invest our money and possessions, and where we will build our lives. For me, where you live is a huge influence on your thinking. The food, accent and language, customs, and societal norms all play a part in shaping and forming you. It's not everything, but it is a thing. More on this in the next chapter on your personal environment.

Faith

Whether you have faith or not, belief is a superpower. Belief is one of the strongest allies you could have in your life. When we believe in something, such as a dream or a cause, it becomes fuel and energy. My faith in God has played a huge role in my life. Because of my faith, I see trials differently. Instead of seeing them as enemies, I see them as working toward perfecting my faith as pure gold. I don't see setbacks as failures but as part of the process of God shaping my character.

Belief will give your pain a purpose. Belief will give rejection meaning and insight. Faith will teach you that all things work together for the good of those who love God (Romans 8:28). It's not the size of the dog in the fight, but it's the size of the fight inside the dog. Your belief is your fight. If you believe you can, you just might.

REFRAME YOUR MIND TO RESHAPE YOUR WORLD

Did you know that thoughts are born twice: first in your mind and then in your life? A thought can actually become physical. For Christians, God isn't only concerned about transforming your heart, He is also interested in renewing your mind. Both heart and mind need to be changed according to His Word and will.

I read this book by author Daniel Coyle titled *The Talent Code*. I recommend that every leader should own a copy of this book. His main theme is that greatness isn't born—it is grown.

My main takeaways from the book are that with deep practice and proper coaching, growth can occur, and you can rewire your current neurological pathways.[13] Why is this important? Because we do things out of memory, so if we can change the memory, we can indeed improve.

Romans 12:2 (NKJV) says, "And do not be conformed to this world, but be transformed by the renewing of your mind, that you may prove what *is* that good and acceptable, and perfect, will of God." We as believers must understand that when we come to Christ in our salvation, our minds have been focused on worldly things. In order for our minds to be renewed and changed, we must be transformed. Reading the Bible—God's Word—is part of that journey. To produce different fruit, we must have different thoughts.

---

13 Daniel Coyle, *The Talent Code: Greatness Isn't Born, It's Grown* (London, England: Random House Business, 2020).

PERSONAL GROWTH IS PERSONAL

Imagine with me a dirt road, and let's say you live on that road. I grew up in a small town, so I know all about these dusty roads. Let's say this is the only road available to get to your house every day. It's bumpy. It's dusty. It's annoying, but you go on it because that is all you have. Now, let's say that a company takes it upon themselves and builds a two-lane road on the other side that is covered with asphalt. They paint yellow lines on it. All of the touches. Since you found out, you now drive on this road to your house. It is no longer bumpy, your car doesn't get dirty from the dust, and it's actually a pleasant experience.

This is the same with our thoughts. Maybe for many years, you have thought the way you do because that is all you have known. But, what if I told you there are better ways of thinking—more redemptive ways of believing?

Your thoughts drive on the pathways that you have created in your mind. James Allen also says, "Let a man radically alter his thoughts, and he will be astonished at the rapid transformation it will effect in the material conditions of his life."[14]

DEVELOPING A WINNING MINDSET

So, what can we do? Don't be afraid. It's okay. Everything will be okay. One step at a time. Building a correct mindset takes time and dedication. Myron Golden, a prolific motivational speaker, says, "Thinking is the hardest work most people never do."[15] The reason is due to the fact that our brain requires lots of energy to think. It has been said that despite the relatively small size of our

---

14 James Allen, *As a Man Thinketh: A Guide to Unlocking the Power of Your Mind*.
15 Myron Golden, Twitter post, November 29, 2023, 12:07 p.m., https://twitter.com/MyronGoldenPhD/status/1729909882013261903.

PERSONAL MINDSET

brain compared to the rest of our body, it can use up to 20 percent of the body's energy.[16]

Have you ever felt exhausted after back-to-back meetings during which you had to contribute, share, and exchange? There is a reason for that. Your brain was working. Lots of people would rather avoid the hard work of thinking because it's easier not to think. It requires fewer calories. If you want to get ahead in life, become a thinker. Think about ideas, solutions, and progress. Think of ways to overcome. This is where Philippians 4:8 (MSG) comes in:

Summing it all up, friends, I'd say you'll do best by filling your minds and meditating on things true, noble, reputable, authentic, compelling, gracious—the best, not the worst; the beautiful, not the ugly; things to praise, not things to curse.

Remember, to change your life, change your mind. Sometimes, that means changing your mind about yourself. See yourself as God sees you. Don't let others see more potential in you than you see in yourself.

> **Don't let others see more potential in you than you see in yourself.**

If you have experienced consecutive seasons of what you would call "losing," be encouraged. You didn't lose; you learned. Change

---

16 "How Your Brain Makes and Uses Energy," *Queensland Brain Institute–University of Queensland*, 28 July 2020, qbi.uq.edu.au/brain/nature-discovery/how-your-brain-makes-and-uses-energy#:~:text=Your%20brain%20is%20arguably%20the,of%20your%20energy%20each%20day.

PERSONAL GROWTH IS PERSONAL

your thinking about it. Losing is a mindset. So is winning. Here are some easy steps to take to begin the renewal process of your mind:

1) *Realize your current mindset.*

This helps you to look within and guides you to think about your thoughts. You have to be honest with yourself. How do you think?

- What do you believe about yourself?
- About others?
- About your future?
- About your past?

Ask yourself these questions and I would encourage you to write down your answers. You will see your perspective. Perhaps talk about your answers with your spouse or a trusted friend. It helps to share and get it out of your heart.

2) *Recognize mental moments from your life.*

This helps you to go back and point out how your mind got shaped the way it did. Go back and do some personal research. You think the way you do for a reason. You didn't arrive here without going through something in life. We all have experienced the following:

- Moments that blessed us.
- Moments that changed us.
- Moments that hurt us.
- Moments that taught us.
- Moments that liberated us.
- Moments that helped us.

Once you do this, reflect. Ask God to cleanse your heart of any hurt. Thank Him for moments that built you and didn't break you. You might even see His hand in chapters in your life you didn't even realize He was there.

3) *Renew your mind according to His Word.* This helps to learn how God thinks by reading the Bible. The mind of God is the Word of God. In order to get His way of thinking, we have to read His thoughts in His Word. See, the Bible is like His DNA. As you read it, you are injecting yourself more and more each time.
- Find a good Bible reading plan.
- Read about Jesus and observe His thinking.
- Memorize Bible verses that can help you in your journey.

Keep a journal so you can write down your thoughts. Use the SOAP method (Scripture, Observation, Application, and Prayer). The goal isn't to read it quickly; it's to read it consistently.

4) *Read insightful content to feed your mind.* This has to do with getting an outside perspective on topics and things other than ourselves. Let's face it—we don't know everything. It takes humility to learn from others. The brain wants to be entertained. Your destiny and future want to be fed.
- Create a book reading list.
- Look for podcasts that you can listen to on topics you want to know more about.
- Join a group that focuses on personal growth.

Books and podcasts are so helpful. We live in the Information Age, and it takes a lot of work not to learn anything these days with so much available to us.

PERSONAL GROWTH IS PERSONAL

5) *Rehearse thoughts of victory—not of defeat.* Think about what you are thinking about. If we are losing in our minds, we will lose in our lives. Let me say this again—losing is a mindset. Winning must be repeated in our minds before we see it in our lives.
   - Write out a declaration concerning your future, such as "I will see the glory of God in my life."
   - Ask God to cast down every mental stronghold in your life.
   - Seek out support from others who can speak into your heart.

   Share small wins with others. Record them in your journal. Testify to others about the goodness of God in your life. Whatever you keep in your heart stays with you, but whatever you give away has the potential to multiply. Plus, you never know how your personal victories will encourage others, no matter how small and insignificant they may seem to you.

6) *Release verbally what you are thinking mentally.* Once your mind begins to evolve, talk about it. Don't suppress the transformation. Again, give your purpose a voice. Give your passion words.
   - Let your conversations be filled with new words.
   - Allow your mouth to speak faith-filled promises.
   - Guard your self-talk and how you talk about yourself and others.
   - Seek to add value rather than tear down.

PERSONAL MINDSET

Your life is the public photograph of what your mind privately captures.

I am going to believe this with you: God is going to remake you. You don't have to stay as you are. And, you don't have to live a life of defeat.

You can overcome.

You can walk in freedom.

You can think better.

Whatever seeds were planted that were not of God, today, we ask the Holy Spirit to uproot them and remove them. Your potential is great, and your future is bright.

I dare you to dream again!

> **PRAYER FOR YOUR PERSONAL MINDSET:**
>
> Father, I thank You for giving me the mind of Christ. If I have been operating with a scarcity mindset or a poverty-driven mindset, forgive me. I do not want to live beneath the grace You have called me to walk in. I ask that through the power of Your Holy Spirit, You would renew my mind and perspectives. Help me to see what I need to see. Rewire my mind. Transform my spirit. Tenderize my heart toward You. I believe I am a victor and not a victim. I believe that I am the head and not the tail. I believe that You are expanding me in this very hour.
>
> In Jesus' name. Amen.

CHAPTER 4

PERSONAL COMMUNICATION

"The number one criteria for advancement and promotion for professionals is an ability to communicate effectively."
— *Harvard Business Review*

"STICKS AND STONES MAY BREAK MY BONES, but words will never hurt me." Do you remember hearing this growing up? I sure do. We would use it as a verbal shield to let someone know that what they were saying would be rendered ineffective the moment it came our way. I am not too sure who came up with that statement, but I think I am going to have to disagree. I kind of chuckle thinking about it now because as you and I have learned and experienced, we remember words well beyond the moment they were spoken.

Words are powerful. Full of life and also full of death. As a matter of fact, Proverbs 18:21 (MSG) says, "Words kill, words give life; they're either poison or fruit—you choose." If you really want to go deeper with a Bible study on words in the book of Proverbs, here are some additional verses to think about:

- Proverbs 10:11 (MSG): "The mouth of a good person is a deep, life-giving well, but the mouth of the wicked is a dark cave of abuse."
- Proverbs 10:19 (NKJV): "In the multitude of words sin is not lacking, But he who restrains his lips is wise."
- Proverbs 10:21 (NKJV): "The lips of the righteous feed many, But fools die for lack of wisdom."

PERSONAL GROWTH IS PERSONAL

There are plenty of other verses in Scripture, but you get the point. What we say matters and I would add, how we say it matters too. Rabbi Steve Leder said the following:

In Hebrew, the word for "word" and the word for "thing" is the same word. . . . You cannot differentiate between a word and a thing. . . . For us, words are real. They are concrete. They can build up, they can tear down. They last. And when you consider your words in that context, you use them differently.[17]

He goes on to say that the phrase "abracadabra" (one you have maybe heard magicians use) is actually an Aramaic phrase which means "I create as I speak."[18] We are creating everything we speak.

The language of growth is more intentional than the language of complacency. Growth-oriented people understand that their words carry meaning and authority. My words are troops dispatched for the purpose I need them to fulfill. They are on my team. A wise author once said, "Repeat anything long enough, and it will start to become you." One of the best ways to know you are around winners and growth-minded individuals is to listen to them. You will never perform at a world-class level with amateur language. And, depending on your background and experiences, your brain programming may need to be reset and reprogrammed to fit where God is taking you. Dr. Shad Helmstetter, in his book

---

17 Meghan Rabbitt, "The One Thing We Have in Common Is Death. Rabbi Steve Leder Shows Us a New Way to Think about Life," *Sunday Paper PLUS*, 11 June 2022, www.mariashriversundaypaper.com/the-one-thing-we-have-in-common-is-death-rabbi-steve-leder-shows-us-a-new-way-to-think-about-life/.
18 Meghan Rabbitt, "The One Thing We Have in Common Is Death. . . ."

PERSONAL COMMUNICATION

What to Say When You Talk To Yourself, says that up to 77 percent of the average person's self-talk is negative.[19]

The more I have talked to people and have helped others develop their potential, the more I recognize how vital the ability to communicate with others and themselves is to a person's growth. People who have impacted your life more than likely did so because of what they said. Maybe it was their book, a speech, a sermon, or a conversation—but, I am pretty confident that it involved some form of communication and words.

By the way, don't be alarmed. I am not asking you to step in front of a huge audience and give a speech. But . . . you will need to speak up for your future and where you believe God has called you to be. That future needs a voice and desires to be expressed. It is looking for a place to thrive and breathe, but if we aren't speaking life-giving words, we could potentially suffocate the greatness within. When I learned the growth mindset, I began to speak growth words. And when I began to speak words directed toward growth, I began to see change and results. When I began to see change and results, I began to speak to others differently. All growth feeds other parts of our lives.

And God has placed within you the authority to have dominion, even over your words.

> **God has placed within you the authority to have dominion, even over your words.**

---

[19] Shad Helmstetter, *What to Say When You Talk to Yourself* (New York, NY: Park Avenue Press, 2011) 11.

PERSONAL GROWTH IS PERSONAL

WORDS LIVE BEYOND

"Mijo, you are going to be somebody when you grow up."

Did I mention that I was adopted by my uncle and aunt when I was an infant? I wasn't raised by my biological parents, and looking back, I can see the hand of God all over my life, even in moments I didn't understand. My father who raised me was a very loving man toward our family. Even though he had his bouts with former struggles throughout his years, he and my mom gave me a childhood with so many great memories. One of the important lessons he taught me was affirmation. He was huge on this, especially toward me.

My father affirmed me throughout my childhood and often spoke great things over my life. He knew before anyone else that I would go on to achieve personal success. He wouldn't have had it any other way. Unfortunately, my father died one month after my wedding. I had never grieved the way I did when he passed away. If you have lost a parent, you know what I am talking about.

Even though he is no longer in this world, his words live on in my life. I truly believe that I have become who I am today by the grace of God and by his words that germinated to life within my heart and mind. Today, I constantly speak blessing over my children. I tell them that God has a special purpose and plan for their lives. I also affirm and speak into other people's lives. You see the ripple effect? Words live. People will often live up to the standards placed over them. And the reason I say this is because beliefs become behavior.

It's important to be a person that is a multiplier of potential and not one that diminishes.

I know that this principle of words living on can work in the good and in the bad. Maybe you are reading this book, and the words that were planted in your heart and mind were negative and belittling. Maybe someone hurt you by what they said about you. Maybe their perception of you and conversations about you haven't been evicted from your self-image.

I know we all have different backgrounds and experiences. Many people will live their lives under a wrong self-image created by another's words. And if they are not careful, they will repeat the same mistake and spread their hurt to someone else.

Before you read on, say this prayer with me:

Father, I come before you asking You to uproot any negative and hurtful word that has been planted in me. I command those roots to wither and fade away. I believe that greater is He that is within me than he that is in the world. I declare my mind is renewed, and my thoughts are restored. In Jesus' name. Amen.

Your words have significance. To continue to reach new heights in your life, your words will need to align with your renewed mind. Let the redeemed of the Lord say so. Moreover, when your mind, mouth, and mission are all moving in the same direction, you become a powerful force. Ralph Waldo Emerson said, "The world makes way for the man who knows where he is going."

MOUTH AND MIND

There are two worlds where communication takes place. First, in you. Second, through you. Self-talk happens all the time. I am not referring to you talking to yourself out loud but what you say to yourself internally on a consistent basis. We all do it, and we do it every day. As a matter of fact, I once said that your internal words are so influential that you can literally talk yourself into or out of something.

And listen, what you say about yourself and to yourself makes a huge difference. My dad thought I would be somebody great, and his words eventually became my thoughts. If you hear something over and over again, you just might believe it, and what you believe, you become. Thoughts become things, and words are the vehicle to carry out their orders.

Some of you reading this book have great talent and a bright future, but your potential hindrance is your communication. It may be that you simply do not have the vocabulary that matches your promises... yet. The Israelites in the Old Testament were delivered by the Lord from Egypt. But, they couldn't renew their thoughts and words to match where they were going. They were so focused on where they had been and lived that it bled through their speech. They made comments like, "Oh, that we had died by the hand of the Lord in the land of Egypt" (Exodus 16:3, NKJV). They also confessed, "For it would have been better for us to serve the Egyptians than that we should die in the wilderness" (Exodus 14:12, NKJV).

Your words frame your world. What you say creates an environment. Hebrews 11:3 (NKJV) says, "By faith we understand that the worlds were framed by the word of God, so that the things which are seen were not made of things which are visible." God's Word framed the world.

Building communication skills doesn't happen overnight, but it can be done over time. A technique that I teach others when it comes to public communication is to teach their mouth to keep up with their mind. A common struggle among novices in public speaking is that their words often sound better in their mind than they do when they actually say them. "It sounded better in my mind," is a common theme I hear. And, yes, I bet it did. But, your mouth has to be "trained" to follow your thoughts and where you are trying to take people. When both your mind and mouth work together, you can achieve great results or at least, communicate what you are trying to convey.

WORDS WITH FRIENDS

So, how can I get better? Let me give you a few ways that you can practice in real-time to help improve your personal communication.

1) *Write.* Buy a journal or a notebook and write. Many times, the reason we aren't clear with our words is because we aren't clear in our minds. A cluttered mind often produces confused communication. Writing is a practice that helps to get your thoughts out of your mind. Write your goals in life. Write what you want to do this week. Write where you want to visit one day. Write your prayers and declarations. Get your thoughts flowing.

2) *Talk.* Yes, talk. Talk to someone. Talk to a friend. Talk to a coach or mentor. Learn the skill of communicating. We learn by doing, and if you want to improve your communication, communicate. I used to be embarrassed of how I read in school, but I overcame it by reading out loud in class. It built my inner courage. Practice with others.

3) *Listen.* You know what has helped me to speak more clearly and communicate more effectively? I have learned the skill

of listening. By listening, you hear what's in people's hearts. You find out what they are searching for and what they lack in their life. You find out what makes them happy and what ignites their passion. Learning is listening.

These are three easy ways to help grow in your communication. Of course, you can do the following:
- Give a public speech.
- Share a Bible study with friends.
- Prepare a presentation for work.
- Pray out loud when requested.
- Take a class on communication.
- Use social media to communicate your message.
- Record a video and watch yourself talk.

The goal isn't perfection—but progress. Jim Rohn said, "If you just communicate, you can get by. But if you can communicate skillfully, you can work miracles."[20]

> **The goal isn't perfection—but progress.**

Your life is a unique story that no one else has. Maybe you're thinking, *Abram, I can understand personal awareness and*

---

[20] Steph Nagl, "The Importance of Strategic Communication Skills in the Digital Age," *School of Professional Studies at Wake Forest University*, 4 May 2023, sps.wfu.edu/articles/communication-skills-in-the-digital-age/#:~:text=Author%20and%20speaker%20Jim%20Rohn,the%20business%20world%20as%20well.

PERSONAL COMMUNICATION

personal mindset, but communication? Not sure how they will help me grow. Trust me; I completely understand. But the reality is your dream needs a voice. What God has placed deep within you needs to find its way out of you into the world it was meant to touch and impact. The enemy's desire is to keep you silent and mute. But I believe that God wants to give birth to your voice. Your personal growth is directly connected to how you talk about yourself and toward others. If you miss this, you may miss other things that are in store for you or, at the very least, delay opportunities. Your perspective and testimony are both angles that no one else sees. I can only see things through my own eyes, but if you share with me your lens, I can see it through your eyes too. Some of you have stories to tell and insights to share. Speak and speak clearly.

> **PRAYER FOR YOUR PERSONAL COMMUNICATION:**
>
> Father, thank You for the power of words. Help me to use my words wisely and purposely. I pray that moving forward from this moment, my mouth would be filled with life and honor and power. Use my mouth to speak Your will and plans. Use my words to add value to others around me. I surrender all that is involved with communication from my life to You. Have Your way, and may every word glorify Your name. I prophesy greatness in my future. I will see the goodness of the Lord in the land of the living. I will declare the praises of Him from one generation to the next generation. In Jesus' name. Amen.

CHAPTER 5

PERSONAL ENVIRONMENT

"Be a yardstick of quality. Some people aren't used to an environment where excellence is expected."
—STEVE JOBS[21]

---

21 Steve Jobs, Motivating Thoughts of Steve Jobs: Learning from the Innovative and Visionary Business Leader (New Delhi, India: Prabhat Prakashan, 2016).

PERSONAL ENVIRONMENT

THERE'S THIS STORY ABOUT ONE OF THE BEST power forwards in basketball who has ever played the game. His name is Tim Duncan. Nicknamed the "Big Fundamental," Tim spent his entire career of nineteen seasons with one team—the San Antonio Spurs. He is a five-time NBA Champion, a two-time NBA MVP, a three-time NBA Finals MVP, a fifteen-time NBA All-Star, and the only player to be selected to both the All-NBA and All-Defensive Teams for thirteen consecutive seasons.

His accolades are plenty, and he experienced no shortage of success. However, it didn't begin that way. At the beginning of his young life, Tim actually aspired to be an Olympic-level swimmer. He was born and raised in Saint Croix, U.S. Virgin Islands. His family consisted of his parents and two older sisters, along with an older brother. His sisters were swimmers, and one of his sisters actually swam for the U.S. Virgin Islands at the 1988 Summer Olympics in Seoul. Like his sister, Tim excelled at swimming and was a teenage standout. With plans to go to the 1992 Olympic Games as a member of the US team, Tim set his bar high and aggressively pursued his goal.

Then, calamity struck.

In 1989, Hurricane Hugo destroyed the island's only Olympic-sized swimming pool, and it forced Tim to swim in the ocean instead. Due to his fear of sharks, he lost complete enthusiasm for swimming. It was actually his brother-in-law who

PERSONAL GROWTH IS PERSONAL

encouraged him to turn to basketball, and that was the turning point in his life. From swimming pools to a basketball gym, Tim's life was radically altered.

We may think that our environment doesn't play a part in our development, but the truth is that it does. Had Tim's pool survived the hurricane, we may not be talking about him as one of the greatest basketball players to play in his position. He probably wouldn't even be mentioned in this book.

One of the key determining influences in your life that helps to shape who you are is the environment you are surrounded by and that you allow yourself to live in. Rather than sit back and do nothing, Tim allowed himself to explore and try something different in a new environment. Here lies a secret superpower: our ability to choose. The hurricane was out of Tim's control, but other decisions—to step into a new environment, to pursue a different sport, and to keep moving forward—were within it.

I understand that there may be some things completely out of your control when it comes to your personal environment. You didn't choose the home you grew up in or the city where your parents decided to live. Perhaps you had to attend a particular high school, and maybe the finances were not there to choose the college of your choice. Again, don't stop there. I also believe that there are some things within your control. You can choose the attitude you will have or the people you will allow in your life. You can choose to be a part of groups or communities that are like-minded. Right now in your life, I am sure there are choices that you have control over.

PERSONAL ENVIRONMENT

> **Here is a truth: you do have a lot of influence on your environment—maybe more than you realize or more than you would like to believe.**

Here is a truth: you do have a lot of influence on your environment—maybe more than you realize or more than you would like to believe.

YOUR ENVIRONMENT MATTERS

I define environment as this:

You + your sphere + the people in your sphere + any other influences you allow in your sphere = your environment

What I am referring to is where you live, where you work, who you hang around with, the type of conversations you dwell among, the music you listen to, the shows you watch, and any other stimulant that fills your personal space. All of it creates environment.

Think about your favorite coffee shop or restaurant. I am sure that one of the reasons you like it is due to the fact that the "vibe" connects with you. If you think environment doesn't matter or affect you, use fluorescent lighting instead of candles for a romantic dinner. Wives, you can thank me later. Just kidding.

Companies have understood the power of environment. Nature understands the power of environment. Not all seeds thrive in the same kind of environment. As a matter of fact, it has been said that plant growth and where the plant can grow are greatly affected by the environment. Environmental factors that affect plant growth include light, temperature, water, humidity, and nutrition.[22]

Pause for a moment. If plants need a good environment to produce fruit, I wonder if we need a good environment to thrive. In this season of our life, we have a pet dog. His name is Duke. My family does its best to ensure that Duke has a good home environment, from where he sleeps at night to his meals to his daily routine of going outside. All of this for a dog. I am sure a lot of dog lovers and owners could and would agree that it takes work to have a dog. Again, if we do this for our pets, why not for ourselves?

My answer—yes. More on this in a moment, but for now, we can turn to the greatest evidence of this truth that will ever be: the Bible.

ENVIRONMENT EXAMPLES

First, let's start in the Old Testament. Although there are several passages I could select, take a look at this verse found in 1 Samuel 16:23 (NKJV):

> *And so it was, whenever the spirit from God was upon Saul, that David would take a harp and play it with his hand. Then Saul would become refreshed and well, and the distressing spirit would depart from him.*

The narrative describes King Saul and his battle with a depressing mood and spirit. David, who had already made an impression upon Saul's team, would be summoned to come into the presence of King

---

[22] Hiroshi Ashihara, et al., "Environmental Factors and Nucleotide Metabolism," *Plant Nucleotide Metabolism Biosynthesis, Degradation, and Alkaloid Formation* (Chichester, United Kingdom: Wiley, 2020).

Saul. And, he would play his instrument—the harp. Now, you know by now that music affects mood and atmosphere.

Try it in your own life. Have you noticed that when you play certain kinds of music, you feel some kind of way? When I want to go for deep study or personal reflection, I play jazz. When I want to spend time in prayer, I will play worship-style music. I have found that it creates an atmosphere that glorifies God and provokes me to want to just spend time with Him. It soothes my soul. I lift up my eyes toward Him. I take my focus off myself. It allows my mind and thoughts to synchronize and align. I regain direction.

All of this is environment.

Secondly, here is a verse that involves Jesus in the New Testament:
Now He could do no mighty work there, except that He laid His hands on a few sick people and healed them. And He marveled because of their unbelief.
—Mark 6:5-6 (NKJV)

He returned back to His hometown and taught them the same way He was teaching others. By this time in His life, He was already walking in His purpose and public ministry. But, something was different about the people and environment. They simply couldn't get over the fact that this was the same Jesus who grew up with them. They knew his parents. They knew His father's occupation and even referenced it. They knew his siblings and probably knew stories of his upbringing. When He began to teach them, they marveled, not with expectancy, but with offense. They couldn't believe (perhaps) that He would think He could teach them a thing or two. Maybe some didn't like him. Whatever it was, it hindered the atmosphere. Just another piece of wisdom for you: the people we allow in our proximity do affect atmosphere. Ever been to a concert, and everybody was as equally excited? You probably didn't just see that; you felt it.

> **Environments often include people—and that one factor makes a HUGE difference.**

And, due to that very fact, Jesus couldn't perform miracles as He did in other towns because of their unbelief. The environment just didn't lend itself to an atmosphere of faith. Try getting around a bunch of naysayers, and share your dreams. See how that goes. Try telling several pessimists your optimistic view of the future, and see how you feel afterward. Environments often include people—and that one factor makes a HUGE difference.

Just to add to the conversation, take a look at what Jesus did when he brought Jairus's daughter back to life in Mark 5:35-43 (NKJV):

> *While He was still speaking, some came from the ruler of the synagogue's house who said, "Your daughter is dead. Why trouble the Teacher any further?"*
>
> *As soon as Jesus heard the word that was spoken, He said to the ruler of the synagogue, "Do not be afraid; only believe." And He permitted no one to follow Him except Peter, James, and John the brother of James. Then He came to the house of the ruler of the synagogue, and saw*

> *a tumult and those who wept and wailed loudly. When He came in, He said to them, "Why make this commotion and weep? The child is not dead, but sleeping."*
>
> *And they ridiculed Him. But when He had put them all outside, He took the father and the mother of the child, and those who were with Him, and entered where the child was lying. Then He took the child by the hand, and said to her, "Talitha, cumi," which is translated, "Little girl, I say to you, arise." Immediately the girl arose and walked, for she was twelve years of age. And they were overcome with great amazement. But He commanded them strictly that no one should know it, and said that something should be given her to eat.*

He didn't permit anyone to follow Him except Peter, James, and John. Also, when He came to the house, He put everyone outside except the parents of the child and the disciples with Him. Why? Environment matters. Look at the story. It says that some of the crowd "ridiculed Him." Sometimes, we have to move on from people who simply don't believe. Dr. Henry Cloud said, "In order to make room for new things that give you hope, you must get rid of old things that are taking up space."[23]

A LEADER'S ECOSYSTEM

If you are going to arrive at your next level, it may be time to assess your current environment. In the beginning, God created

---

[23] Henry Cloud, Twitter post, November 25, 2023, 5:48 p.m., https://twitter.com/DrHenryCloud/status/1728546102985609613.

the heavens and the earth. He also created an environment called the Garden of Eden. Within this garden, He placed everything needed for His creation to survive and thrive. The Scriptures mention that the garden was filled with trees that were pleasant to the sight and good for food, and, there was a river that went out of Eden to water the garden, and it continued from there to become four riverheads (Genesis 2).

> **If you are going to arrive at your next level, it may be time to assess your current environment.**

Make a note that this river from the garden would flow from this environment to water other places beyond the garden. Let me stop to add this: there should be a flow from your life. And, that flow should continue from your life and proceed to "water" other places in your world as well as other people. It was never meant to stop with you. You are not a reservoir but a current of blessing. Jesus said, "He who believes in Me, as the Scripture has said, out of his heart will flow rivers of living water" (John 7:38, NKJV).

The garden was not left alone, however. The Bible states in Genesis 2:15 (NKJV), "Then the Lord God took the man and put him in the Garden of Eden to tend and keep it." Adam was placed there to steward this environment. To do work. Work isn't something evil but something good for man as it gives us a sense of responsibility and purpose. Two things we all need: relationships and responsibilities (people and purpose). The Lord placed Adam to take command and authority over this environment that was created. Today, He still expects us to take command and authority over our environment. You have been placed where you are for perhaps a much deeper reason than you have been led to believe.

I know. You might be thinking that Adam had an advantage because he was literally placed in paradise. Okay, two more quick examples. Ezekiel and Titus. Both figures in the Bible were placed in less-than-ideal environments, yet they were expected to produce positive change. Ezekiel was placed in a valley of dry bones, according to Ezekiel 37. There was no life. There were no signs of movement. There was no army. Yet, he was planted there and asked a simple question, "Son of man, can these bones live?" (Ezekiel 37:3, NIV). Rather than complain or wonder, *Why me?* Ezekiel submitted to his assignment and spoke life in his context and environment. Titus 1:5 (NKJV) says that Titus was sent by the apostle Paul to the island of Crete and that he "should set in order the things that are lacking." What was the difference? The person within the environment. You may not have an ideal situation, but let the environment you wish to see in your life exist within who you are.

Let me take you on a quick exercise. Do the following: grab a sheet of paper and jot down some answers to the categories. Write who and what.

1) Your Job—what you currently do
2) Friends—whom you are currently connected with
3) Mentors/Coaches—whom you are currently learning from
4) Music—what you currently listen to

PERSONAL GROWTH IS PERSONAL

5) Room/Office/Space—where you currently work from
6) Community/Region—where you currently live
7) Tools/Books/Other—what you currently use to grow and develop

This isn't an exhaustive list, but something to get you started and thinking. Take a look at your current environment. Notice what you do within that environment: how you live, who you have allowed in, and your daily influences. All of this will make a difference in the long run.

You may be pleased. You may feel what's the point. You may ask yourself, *Can it get better?* You may feel a bit indifferent. All of it is okay. But, if you desire to grow and change, sometimes, things in your surroundings need to change.

> **If you desire to grow and change, sometimes, things in your surroundings need to change.**

If you want to study more, place more books around you. If you want to be healthier, do away with foods you know aren't good for you. If you want to be closer to God, keep your journal and Bible nearby and a good worship playlist. If you want to meet new people, look for places to do so. Again, you can choose, and you can make different decisions.

PERSONAL ENVIRONMENT

Just a tip: creating a place in your home or space for your passion is helpful. In other words, use your walls to speak to you. Use your desk space to guide you. Keep things around you to remind you of a greater future. Maybe it's a vision board. Maybe it's a picture of your family and your dreams. Perhaps it's a note someone gave you that believed in you. Again, give your future self (when you feel discouraged) encouragement to keep going. Build a firewall of protection around your destiny.

I have learned that what is on the inside will eventually make its way toward the outside.

> **PRAYER FOR YOUR PERSONAL ENVIRONMENT:**
>
> Thank You, Lord, that You have protected me so far. Your hand has been on my life, and I didn't even know it. You have guarded, persevered, and provided for me in ways that I will never understand. I pray that You will continually fill my environment with good things. I rebuke anything that does not belong, and I renounce things I should not have let in. Deliver me from any evil I have caused. Thank You for cleansing my life and my atmosphere. I submit to Your will and ways.
> In Jesus' name. Amen.

CHAPTER 6

PERSONAL RELATIONSHIPS

"As iron sharpens iron, so one person sharpens another."
—Proverbs 27:17 (NIV)

PERSONAL RELATIONSHIPS

GROWING UP, I ATTENDED A VERY SMALL SCHOOL from grades kindergarten through twelfth grade. Let me put it to you this way—my graduating class was only thirty-seven people. I know, right? But, you want to know something pretty cool? I was ranked third in my class, which means I made the top 10 percent! Okay, moving on. . . .

My personal experience pretty much involved the same friends and cast of characters throughout my education tenure. The kids who started their journey in kindergarten with me were many of the same ones who completed high school with me. Some moved away throughout our journey. Others joined us during junior high and high school. But, for the most part, it was the same core collective of kids who remained together.

We went to school together. We played sports together. We rode bikes together. You name it—many of us became good friends. There were a few of them that I was really close to in friendship. In those seasons and as you are growing up, you kind of think that it will always be that way. Little did I know that once I graduated high school, things would change radically.

And so would relationships.

For starters, when you graduate high school, everyone has to begin to choose their own path. Whether that is continuing their education, going to work full-time, or pursuing some other venture, life places you at a crossroads. What you want to do and

PERSONAL GROWTH IS PERSONAL

where you want to further your development are two big questions that many students have to answer if they want to pursue the collegiate route. I often get asked by students at the church that I currently serve, "Where do you think would be a good place for me to go to college?" Why? Because it is a big decision that could affect your entire life.

Back in 1997, I had made up my mind that I was going to continue with my education and attend a nearby community college to begin my pursuit in the medical field. I had received scholarships and financial support to begin the journey. This was the point where many other friends of mine began to distance and separate themselves from me. Why? Because we were all going in different directions. Two of my closest friends attended the same college as me, and after a year, they even began to go different ways.

To think that you will always have the same cast of characters in your life in every season is wishful thinking but not realistic. And even if you do, their role in your life may change. I am a parent, and I know that eventually, my kids will choose their own way one day. It's a part of the cycle of life. Rather than fight against the current of growth and change, I have chosen to fully embrace and extrapolate all that relationships provide for me in any given season.

On your personal growth journey, you will see that relationships play a huge part in every area of your life. Dr. Dharius Daniels wrote a great book on relationships called *Relational Intelligence,* and in it, he stated the following:

PERSONAL RELATIONSHIPS

Every single area of your life is inevitably impacted by your relationships. Your spiritual, physical, financial, emotional, and professional progress is tied and tethered to who you allow to be a part of and influence your life. Therefore, if you are serious about taking your life to the next level, you should be serious about taking your relationships to the next level.[24]

In other words, relationships matter. They are consequential. They affect you—good or bad. They help or hinder you.

> **Relationships matter. They are consequential. They affect you—good or bad. They help or hinder you.**

Had I wanted to maintain my friendships with high school buddies with the same proximity that we had in prior seasons, I would have missed what life would present me in my own personal path. I have learned and now I teach others that as you pursue your growth, calling, and career—you will also need to choose relationships. Because not everyone is going in the same direction as you.

Jim Rohn is often cited as the source for this quote, "You're the average of the five people spend the most time with." I feel that

---

[24] Dharius Daniels, *Relational Intelligence: The People Skills You Need for the Life of Purpose You Want* (Grand Rapids, MI: Zondervan, 2020) 13.

there is truth to this statement, although the influence of people in your life may go beyond just five people. Even the apostle Paul told the people of Corinth in 1 Corinthians 15:33 (NIV), "Do not be misled: 'Bad company corrupts good character.'"

If bad company can corrupt good character, which affects behavior, then we must believe that good company can affect behavior as well, including character. Or at least, expose us to something different. Here is another growth equation:

company affects character affects choices

The company you keep can affect your character which can alter your choices. Everything is connected to each other.

FRIENDS AND FUTURE

There is this old adage that says, "Show me your friends, and I'll show you your future." This is another statement that I find great value in. If people can influence you today, they can affect your future. If you hang around people who are doing nothing with their lives and have no goals for their lives, run. Just kidding. But seriously—rethink your relationships. Why? Because their lack of ambition, urgency, and future will affect you in some way, shape, or form. Paul told Timothy, "Flee also youthful lusts; but pursue righteousness, faith, love, peace with those who call on the Lord out of a pure heart" (2 Timothy 2:22, NKJV). Emphasis on the "with those." In other words, find your tribe and people who want the same thing you want. And by the way, just because they are family doesn't mean you aren't capable of making your own decisions. You can decide to grow and reach your full potential.

PERSONAL RELATIONSHIPS

So, do you just cut everyone off from one day to the next? Well, that might be a tension. And, it may not be that easy. I am not suggesting to be rude, arrogant, or distant. I am proposing, though, to shift the weight of value from those who aren't going in the same direction as you toward those who are. You can be friendly without being best friends.

And, here is another piece of advice if you want to join others moving in a direction you see yourself: cultivate those relationships. In other words, you will have to do your part in building relationships with people. Don't expect people to reach out to you through your DMs or in person. You might have to be the one that initiates a conversation, a lunch meeting, or some type of way for you to get connected. The proof of your desire is in your pursuit. You will never possess what you aren't willing to pursue. You are not alone. There are people like you who want to do better, want to serve God, want to fulfill their purpose, understand your journey, and can add great benefit to your life. This just might be the season to venture out and trust God.

In my own growth journey, there have been several key people who have helped to change my life and my future. They have believed in my potential and have even paved the way for me with their sincere prayers, unrelenting support, and key introductions to other people I wouldn't have met without them. I would not be where I am today without them. I am not a self-made man but the product of God's grace, God's favor, and His people whom He has surrounded me with in different seasons. Thank you to my wife, Rebecca, and my family. Thank you, Pastors Jaime and Rose Mary Loya. Thank you, Pastors Peter and Claudia Zarate,

PERSONAL GROWTH IS PERSONAL

and to all those who have spoken words of life into me. You are not forgotten. I carry you in my heart.

> **I am not a self-made man but the product of God's grace, God's favor, and His people whom He has surrounded me with in different seasons.**

There's this story in the Bible found in 2 Kings 3 where the kings of Judah, Israel, and Edom are about to go into battle against the Moabite king. This was initiated because the opposing king essentially rebelled against one of the first kings. You following? Good. Let's continue. So, after some days of frustration, the three kings needed some answers. And here is how that dialogue goes:

But Jehoshaphat said, "Is there no prophet of the Lord here, that we may inquire of the Lord by him?"

So one of the servants of the king of Israel answered and said, "Elisha the son of Shaphat is here, who poured water on the hands of Elijah."

And Jehoshaphat said, "The word of the Lord is with him." So the king of Israel and Jehoshaphat and the king of Edom went down to him.

Then Elisha said to the king of Israel, "What have I to do with you? Go to the prophets of your father and the prophets of your mother."

PERSONAL RELATIONSHIPS

But the king of Israel said to him, "No, for the Lord has called these three kings together to deliver them into the hand of Moab."

And Elisha said, "As the Lord of hosts lives, before whom I stand, surely were it not that I regard the presence of Jehoshaphat king of Judah, I would not look at you, nor see you. But now bring me a musician."
—2 Kings 3:11-15 (NKJV)

Did you catch it? The prophet Elisha made a strong statement. He basically says that if it weren't for his relationship with Jehoshaphat and his regard for him, he wouldn't have even considered a request. But, because of this relationship, Elisha gives wisdom and direction. This would lead to a victory for the three kings!

Could it be possible that your next open door and opportunity is wrapped up in the form of a relationship? But, if we don't see relationships as having value or meaning, we will overlook people when people are the key to other people, and people are part of your purpose. And if we don't make intentional efforts to get around those people, even when it's hard and takes work, then we may not move forward. To be in certain rooms and around certain people, you may have to pay a price. You may have to invest money or resources. You may have to humble yourself and reach out. You may have to book a trip or pay an entrance fee. But again, if you see yourself as valuable, being around value is a part of the process.

PERSONAL GROWTH IS PERSONAL

People often come into our lives for a reason and for a season. Very few people will be with you on your entire journey of life. And if they are and they have served you well, be grateful. They are gifts. Your destiny could very well be connected to theirs. Or perhaps they continually possess the fertilizer you need to keep growing in your own life.

You could be the most talented person at your job, in your sphere, or in your church or group, but if you don't learn to harness and manage your relationships, you could be hindered in your growth. In every stage and season of my life and calling, I have been blessed and fortunate by good relationships. I have also sought and cultivated these relationships. For relationships to be fruitful in their season, here are some things I do to maximize them:

1) *I understand what kind of relationship it is.* Not all relationships carry the same weight and value. Some people will be friends. Some people will be associates. Some people will be assignments. Having relational awareness has helped me to know where that person stands in my life. I wear different hats, so I play different roles.

2) *I understand the law of give and take.* Relationships must be cultivated and developed. Some people only take from others, but they never give back. If you want people to listen to you, you must listen to them. If you want people to affirm you, you must affirm them. Seek not to make the relationship all about you, but seek how you can help them as well. Nurture, don't drain.

3) *I understand that relationships evolve and can change.* Nothing stays the same. We are constantly moving through life. Who you see today, you may not see tomorrow. Who is distant today, may be close tomorrow. You may meet new people. You may stay around the same people. You might change your mind. They might change their mind. Again, life is moving.

These mental insights have helped me gain traction. Let me say this—the writing of this book was because of a relationship. Meeting my hero, John Maxwell, was because of a relationship. Understanding relationships can help you in achieving all that you feel God has called you to do.

THE TYPES OF PEOPLE YOU NEED

There are many articles that you can find on the internet that tell you what kind of people you need in your life. There are people way smarter than me that can guide you in this area. But, I want to add my portion and thoughts on the topic. I am going to give you three types of people using Biblical figures that you should have in your life.

For starters, everyone needs a Barnabas in their life. Barnabas was first introduced to us in Acts 4. He is known as an early supporter and leader in the church. He was also the individual that grabbed Paul by the proverbial hand and gave him credibility among the other disciples. His name means "son of encouragement." Why do we need a Barnabas? Because life is full of challenges, adversity, trials, and other things that you can't predict.

PERSONAL GROWTH IS PERSONAL

This type of person is the kind of person that encourages you and supports you. They are somewhat of a cheerleader for your dreams and ideas. These people can be family members, spouses, friends, and even coworkers. A Barnabas can pick you up when you feel down, take up for you behind your back, become a confidant to you in your journey, and also be called an associate.

Secondly, everyone needs a Paul in their life. Paul was the greatest apostle of the New Testament. He wrote two-thirds of the New Testament and impacted many areas for the mission of Christ. He discipled, led, and instructed lots of believers and disciples. His impact on this world is still felt today. But why do you need a Paul? Because you don't know everything about everything. You and I are just one person with a limited mind of knowledge and experience. We need the help, wisdom, and leadership of others to help us get to our personal next level. Whether it be financial or professional, relational or spiritual—we often need coaches and mentors to help us become all that we are meant to be. Pauls in our life may not necessarily cheerlead us along the way, but they will consult, coach, and even correct us in the journey. Who demands excellence from you? Who confronts you when you are doing wrong? Who teaches you a better way? These are questions for improvement. A Paul may be a pastor, supervisor, or coach in your life. These people show they believe in you by showing you how you can improve. They could also be called advisors.

Lastly, everyone needs a Timothy in their life. Timothy was another figure in the New Testament who was discipled and mentored. He showed great potential but needed the guidance of others (namely Paul) to help bring out the best in him. As a matter of fact, two letters in the New Testament are written specifically to him. Why do you need a Timothy? Because it's not all about you. Having Timothys in your life shows you a much bigger picture. What good is it to become the best and not help others? Not serve others? Your gift and potential are meant to be a blessing to other people. No man or woman is an island. We are all connected in this world, and what we do for others matters. Someone once took time to invest in you. Someone once called greatness out in you. And if they didn't, it doesn't matter. You can do that for someone else. They can also be called assignments.

So, who is your Barnabas? Who is your Paul? Who is your Timothy?

Still think relationships don't matter? They do, and they affect you more than you may realize. Something positive? You can assess and be aware beginning today. "How can I be aware," you may ask. Well, for starters, don't get discouraged if you don't have anyone that fills those slots. It will be fine. You'll be fine. Sometimes, those people are hidden in plain sight; we just don't know how to view them. Other times, they haven't been introduced yet because we haven't been seeking those relationships. Now that you are becoming more aware, your eyes may open to the possibilities. Pray for them in your life. Pray them into your life. Ask God to guide you and point you in the right direction.

> **Don't beat yourself up for anything you didn't know in the past. The point of your growth journey is exactly that—growth.**

PERSONAL GROWTH IS PERSONAL

Don't beat yourself up for anything you didn't know in the past. The point of your growth journey is exactly that—growth. Choose to be a person of value so that you can also add value to others along the way.

> ### PRAYER FOR YOUR PERSONAL RELATIONSHIPS:
>
> Father, I give You honor and glory for the relationships You have placed in my life that have blessed me. You are gracious. I thank You for the new people You are bringing into my path. Open my eyes that I may recognize them. You hold the keys to my future, and I trust Your steps for my life. May every person that You have destined for me to meet bear fruit in my future for Your honor and glory. Give me the strength to remove any relationship that does not belong or give You honor and glory. I receive Your grace and mercy.
> In Jesus' name. Amen.

CHAPTER 7

PERSONAL HABITS

"The difference between who you are and
who you want to be is what you do."
—Bill Phillips

PERSONAL HABITS

WHEN WRITING TO THE CHURCH IN CORINTH, the apostle Paul used startling imagery. A passage of scripture that particularly stands out to me is found in 1 Corinthians 9:24-27 (NKJV):

> Do you not know that those who run in a race all run, but one receives the prize? Run in such a way that you may obtain it. And everyone who competes for the prize is temperate in all things. Now they do it to obtain a perishable crown, but we for an imperishable crown. Therefore I run thus: not with uncertainty. Thus I fight: not as one who beats the air. But I discipline my body and bring it into subjection, lest, when I have preached to others, I myself should become disqualified.

In the first century, sporting events were huge, just as they are in our own time. We live in a culture where sports dominate major cities and are often huge for ratings and local economies. Paul's use of this language was very meaningful to the Corinthians because their city was the center for the Isthmian Games, second in prestige to the ancient Olympics. And if you know of any great athletes, you know that they often have different standards of training, personal disciplines, and habits that separate them from others.

PERSONAL GROWTH IS PERSONAL

Look at some of the GOATS (greatest of all time) in their fields—Michael Jordan, Tom Brady, and Lionel Messi, to name a few. In any particular field of life, for the ones who go on to experience great success, it is often due to the decisions and habits that separate them from the rest. Paul could see this in the first-century athletes. This is why he often encouraged Christian believers to follow the same mindset when it came to the things of God.

> **If you are going to become who God has called you to be, your personal habits will play a role.**

If you are going to become who God has called you to be, your personal habits will play a role.

WHAT ARE HABITS?

Habits are the disciplines, decisions, and routines that you do because you thought of them until they became the things that you do without thinking about them. Let me repeat myself—habits are what you do until you become what you continually do. I see the habit equation like this in my mind:

Being before doing while doing shapes being

I like the way James Clear explains it, author of the book *Atomic Habits*. He says:

> *To a large degree, your identity emerges out of your habits. It's like a self-improvement feedback loop. The*

PERSONAL HABITS

more you repeat a behavior, the more you reinforce the identity associated with that behavior. And the more you reinforce the identity, the more natural it will feel to repeat the behavior.[25]

In other words, when people think of habits, they think of what they want to do—the outcomes. "I want to get closer to God." "I want to grow my potential." "I want to lose weight." "I want to have lots of money." But, they hardly think of who they desire to become. Clear teaches that a person should focus on what they want to become, not just on what they want to achieve. If we don't shift the belief behind the behavior, the habit will only be temporary.

For example, the goal should not be to get good grades but to become a person that studies every day. The goal should not be to write a book but to become a writer. The goal should not be to just pray 2-3 days a week but to become a person that continually seeks after God. The more you do, the more you begin to believe that you are that type of person.

As I have previously mentioned, I received my call to preach at nineteen years old. I knew that I wanted to be a man of God. So, I began to do the things that I saw other great men of God do. Pray, read my Bible, study the Bible, and surround myself with people that were seeking after God. The more I did these spiritual habits and disciplines, the more I felt like I was separated for God's use. It worked the same in 2011 when I knew I wanted to reach my

---

[25] James Clear, *Atomic Habits: An Easy & Proven Way to Build Good Habits & Break Bad Ones: Tiny Changes, Remarkable Results* (London, England: Cornerstone Press, 2022).

PERSONAL GROWTH IS PERSONAL

full potential. I wanted to be a person of growth. So, I began to do the things that learners and growers do—put together a personal growth plan, read books, associate with other learners, and take classes and courses. Once I did these things continually, it only reinforced who I desired to be.

One more quote from James Clear: "Every action you take is a vote for the type of person you wish to become."[26] By the way, you should stop right now and go to Amazon or Barnes and Noble and purchase his book. You'll be glad that you did.

You see, every time you do something habitually, it is a vote. A vote for the type of person you want to become. Every time you go to the gym, you are voting to become a healthier person. Every time you go to church, you are voting to become a committed Christian. Every time you say no to sinful temptation, you are voting to become a righteous person. Every time you pick up a book to read, you are voting to become a person who learns and grows. Every time you save money on unnecessary expenses and invest it in your savings, you are voting to become a wealthier person.

When what you want to be and what you do are walking together in agreement, you are simply being who you are based on doing what you know.

Got it?

> **When what you want to be and what you do are walking together in agreement, you are simply being who you are based on doing what you know.**

---

[26] James Clear, *Atomic Habits: An Easy & Proven Way to Build Good Habits & Break Bad Ones*.

JESUS AND HABITS

I love the fact that Jesus knew who He was and His mission in life at a very early age. We see this in the Gospel according to Luke. The setting is Jerusalem at the time of the Feast of the Passover. Jesus was twelve years old and attended the feast with His parents as was His custom (their family habit). The Bible says that when the days of the feast had finished, Jesus lingered behind in Jerusalem without His parents knowing about it. When they couldn't find Him, they returned to Jerusalem, and this is what they found, according to Luke 2:46-49 (NKJV):

> *Now so it was that after three days they found Him in the temple, sitting in the midst of the teachers, both listening to them and asking them questions. And all who heard Him were astonished at His understanding and answers. So when they saw Him, they were amazed; and His mother said to Him, "Son, why have You done this to us? Look, Your father and I have sought You anxiously."*
>
> *And He said to them, "Why did you seek Me? Did you not know that I must be about My Father's business?"*

Jesus had such a strong sense of purpose. One of my prayers over my children is that they would discover and know their purpose as early as possible, so they can spend the rest of their lives unpacking that purpose. If you are a parent, you should do the same.

Because of His strong sense of purpose and identity, Jesus also had habits that supported who He knew Himself to be. Check out some of these verses that pertain to Jesus and His customs. I like to call them habits:

PERSONAL GROWTH IS PERSONAL

- Luke 4:16 (NKJV): "So He came to Nazareth, where He had been brought up. And as His custom was, He went into the synagogue on the Sabbath day, and stood up to read."
- Matthew 26:55 (NKJV): "In that hour Jesus said to the multitudes, 'Have you come out, as against a robber, with swords and clubs to take Me? I sat daily with you, teaching in the temple, and you did not seize Me.'"
- Luke 5:16 (NKJV): "So He Himself often withdrew into the wilderness and prayed."

He went weekly to the synagogue. He sat daily and taught. He withdrew often to pray. He also had a habit of training others. Want to be more like Christ? Study what He did, and you can with the help of the Holy Spirit. Personal growth, to me, isn't separate from spiritual growth. As a matter of fact, self-development isn't complete development apart from my devotion to Christ. My development submits to His transformation within me.

Augustine wrote in *Confessions*, in AD 400, "How can you draw close to God when you are far from your own self?" Whew. He also prayed, "Grant, Lord, that I may know myself that I may know thee." I would submit to you that we do not find our true self by seeking it. Rather, we find it by seeking God. David Benner, in his book *The Gift of Being Yourself*, wrote this phrase, "Nothing is more important, for if we find our true self we find God, and if we find God, we find our most authentic self."[27] He also stated, "We

---

27 David G. Benner, *The Gift of Being Yourself: The Sacred Call to Self-Discovery* (Downers Grove, IL: IVP Books, 2015) 11.

should never be tempted to think that growth in Christ-likeness reduces our uniqueness."[28]

Chew on that for a minute.

WHO DO YOU WANT TO BE?

So, now the real question—who do you want to be when you grow up? Right now, even my kids can answer this one! But truthfully—who do you want to become? This is where habit-forming begins: identifying who you desire to become.

> **This is where habit-forming begins: identifying who you desire to become.**

What brings you joy? What gives you a sense of purpose? When do you feel most alive? What activities create a flow in you? For me, writing and producing content gets my energy going and my thoughts moving in a singular direction. What activities do you dread? What do you feel is missing from your life? What breaks your heart? What grieves you? These are just a few questions you can ask yourself for personal discovery.

I came across an article that was titled, "9 Habits of Highly Successful People, From a Man Who Spent 5 Years Studying Them." In this article, it stated that these were the nine habits:

1) They get up early.
2) They read, a lot.

---
[28] David G. Benner, *The Gift of Being Yourself: The Sacred Call to Self-Discovery*, 17.

PERSONAL GROWTH IS PERSONAL

3) They spend 15 to 30 minutes each day on focused thinking.
4) They make exercise a priority.
5) They spend time with people who inspire them.
6) They pursue their own goals.
7) They get enough sleep.
8) They have multiple incomes.
9) They avoid time-wasters.[29]

This is a pretty good list that has led to some great results. What we do determines what we become. Someone once said that "thoughts produce acts, acts produce habits, and habits produce character." Whoever made this statement was on to something.

When I knew I wanted to be a person of growth and leadership, here are some things I did:

1) I created a personal growth plan and do this yearly.
2) I read lots of books on leadership and growth.
3) I wrote in my journals. I have a collection of them.
4) I gave myself time to think. Thoughts become things.
5) I practiced gratitude. I am grateful for all that God has done.
6) I invested money into my growth.

Now, over a decade since I created these habits in my life, I have seen tremendous progress. I would encourage you to write your own list of habits you want to create.

Get a blank sheet of paper and just write. Dream. Envision. Set goals. Let your heart pour out.

---

[29] Marguerite Ward, "9 Habits of Highly Successful People, from a Man Who Spent 5 Years Studying Them," *CNBC*, 28 Mar. 2017, www.cnbc.com/2017/03/28/9-habits-of-highly-successful-people.html.

Do me a favor, though: don't get overwhelmed. You can do this. Give yourself time to think. Pray. Talk with someone. With God, all things are possible. Oh, He can also break any stronghold in your life. Ask the Holy Spirit to set you free.

He can cast down strongholds (mental, emotional, etc.) that have dominated your patterns and habits for years. When you believe right, you behave righteously. As you read this right now, my prayer is that God would remove any habits that are hindering your future from your mind and life and that He would restore anything that has been robbed from you.

The Lord is faithful.

> **PRAYER FOR OUR PERSONAL HABITS:**
>
> Father, break any stronghold in my life that is hindering me from pursuing Your purpose. I ask that you help me overcome habits that have been planted for years, and break them into pieces. With the guidance of Your Holy Spirit, I believe You are leading me into righteous habits. Stir up the gift in me and fan the flame. I am called to more. Use my daily routines to bring me closer to You and toward my destiny.
>
> In Jesus' name. Amen.

CHAPTER 8

PERSONAL GROWTH

"Don't wish it was easier, wish you were better. Don't wish for less problems, wish for more skills. Don't wish for less challenge, wish for more wisdom."
—J<small>IM</small> R<small>OHN</small>

PERSONAL GROWTH

I WANT YOU TO KNOW THAT YOU CAN GROW. You don't have to stay in the same place mentally, physically, or spiritually.

The Lord has designed His plans for your life that often include all the elements that we wish were not a part of the journey. Rejection, loneliness, criticism, negativity, failure, and so much more can often discourage us from moving forward. Yet, His grace is always sufficient.

There comes a time when learning must turn into action. After all, action is where change begins to take place. Listening. Learning. Reading. Understanding. Watching. All helpful and often necessary for our own personal comprehension. But for all the books I have read and teachings I have heard, I knew that was only half of it. I also needed to apply what I was learning, or else it stayed internal—on a shelf collecting dust. The anointing over your life is activated when you serve others with your gift.

Personal growth is personal. It doesn't matter if you buy all the books in the world. If application isn't part of your process, you might be very knowledgeable, but isn't transformation a goal? The goal?

For a Christian, sermons and Bible studies should turn into a lifestyle.

For an athlete, watching game films and studying others should turn into an improved game. For a doctor, lectures and residency

PERSONAL GROWTH IS PERSONAL

should turn into an effective practice helping as many patients as possible. Even Jesus knew that His disciples would eventually need to live without Him physically present.

I cannot grow for you. Your mentor cannot grow for you. Your favorite author or hero cannot grow for you. It's personal.

> **I cannot grow for you. Your mentor cannot grow for you. Your favorite author or hero cannot grow for you. It's personal.**

I have encountered lots of people over the years who assume growth will automatically happen in their lives. As they get older. As they attend more conferences. As they breathe. But, they soon find out that is simply not the case. A person must participate in their own growth and experience the stretching that comes from it.

As I shared in the first chapter, my very first growth plan included the following:
1) Read twenty-four books.
2) Listen to one podcast a week.
3) Meet with a new person every week.

I did this back in 2012, and I haven't stopped putting together a plan to grow since that season. They say the best time to plant a tree was ten years ago. The second best time to plant a tree is right now. With that being said, there is no sense in looking back at what you haven't done. Let's focus on what you can do beginning today.

PERSONAL GROWTH MYTHS

Let me establish some myths that I believe that people have when it comes to personal growth. Maybe these have hindered you in your journey.

1) *The older I get, the better I get.*

This may be true in some cases and in certain areas, but it's definitely not true in all cases and all areas. Growth is an intentional decision you make. When your annual birthday comes around, it is simply announcing another year of your life. What it doesn't guarantee is that you became wiser, better, improved, or transformed.

The future does promise you one thing—you will get older, but it doesn't promise that you will get better. Unless, you decide to.

2) *I wasn't born a leader, so growth isn't for me.*

The truth is—no one is born a leader. Greatness isn't born; it is developed. Growth is for anyone and everyone. Just as people can grow in their faith, so can people grow in their gifts. You can grow in your understanding of money, relationships, and any other topic you are interested in. Growth isn't limited to a certain group of people—it is available to all. You don't have to be great to start, but you do have to start to be great.

PERSONAL GROWTH IS PERSONAL

3) *I've made too many mistakes, so growth is behind me.*

We all have made mistakes. Join the club. I've made so many mistakes over the years, I've lost count. But, mistakes don't have to be the end of your growth. Failure doesn't have to be fatal or final. Failure is not an identity. You can grow from your mistakes and learn from them. And I choose to believe that God has a way of redeeming everything in your life for His goodness.

4) *Others are better than me, so growth is beyond me.*

Comparison will keep you from reaching your personal best. Comparison will take your eyes off what God has given you and focus on what others have. You'll forget about your gifts and wish you had their gifts. Again, this is a myth. You have a gift, and you have a grace. Others might be better than you, but did you stop to think that it could be because they are developing themselves? Maybe they have dedicated themselves to their craft. Rather than wish, cultivate growth in your life.

5) *I am already established, so growth is beneath me.*

I once heard a great leader say, "When you stop growing, you stop leading." You have to decide in your heart that you are going to be a lifelong learner. No one has all the answers, and no one knows everything. We learn from others. We learn from experiences. We learn in the journey. Even as smart as you are today, you can still grow. By the way, there are several areas to grow in as well.

SO HOW CAN YOU GROW?

I know . . . growth can seem like this giant sitting in your room taunting you to do something already. But I promise you—it's not. Growth is your friend. Your personal growth is the gift that keeps on giving. Rather than being intimidated by it, lean into it. Dive into it. Meet it head-on. Remember, personal growth is personal.

> **Growth is your friend. Your personal growth is the gift that keeps on giving. Rather than being intimidated by it, lean into it. Dive into it. Meet it head-on.**

Let me share with you some practical ways that you can grow and what it could look like in real life. I mentioned the importance of seeking out mentors in chapter 3, so I want to reiterate here that every suggested step will come with more ease if you have mentors/coaches in your life. I cannot stress enough the importance of connecting with people further down the road than you. If you want to grow in an area of your life—find a person who can help you grow in that area. Health, marriage, finances, faith—you name it. Build a growth team—people you can go to for certain things that are helping you further your life.

1) *Place a time on your daily and weekly schedule for personal growth.*

   If it's not on the schedule, it doesn't exist. This is a mantra I have lived by for years. Just like you make time for your

PERSONAL GROWTH IS PERSONAL

work, your fun, and whatever other priorities you may have, you have to make time for personal growth and development. Otherwise, it may never happen. You will not stumble into success. Pick a day(s) out of your week—no matter how much time you can dedicate to it—and do it. Schedule your growth.

2) *Build a desired reading list, and invest in books.*

You may not be a reader . . . yet. I think it's because you may not know where to start, or you just haven't read the right book yet! There is hope. Whether you prefer audio or hard copy, begin to identify what books you would like to have in your collection. Build your personal library. Right now is the time to learn anything about everything.

3) *Watch self-improvement videos that can add value to you and your growth.*

I would include good biblical teachings in this group as well. Faith comes by hearing the Word of God (Romans 10:17). It's hard to build yourself when all you are allowing to enter into your heart and mind is entertainment. Nothing wrong with it, but it may not be edifying. We can get lost in scrolling and binge-watching. Consider finding some good YouTube channels or teachings on topics you want to learn more about. There are some great teachers out there with valuable insight and grace.

4) *Attend seminars and conferences that can inspire you.*

I would encourage you to get away from your normal weekly routine a few times a year and go learn from others. Step into an environment that will be catered for growth.

Many companies and organizations do this for their teams because they see the value in it. If you are a leader of a team, consider doing this for your people. Growth is the gift that keeps on giving. Lots of churches host great conferences. John Maxwell and other great speakers often put together seminars geared for growth. Find one that you want to attend and go.

5) *Listen to helpful podcasts on a weekly basis.*

This is something you can do on your commute to work or between errands. Rather than listening to music, try listening to a podcast. There is a plethora of podcasts on any given topic. I listen to several during different seasons that speak to me and provide fresh wisdom for my life. It's free and easy to do. Sometimes, the things that are easiest to do are often not done because they are easy not to do as well.

These are five helpful ideas to help you get started, but as you grow, you will create your own path. Traveling, doing new things, spending time with your spouse, going back to school, learning a new craft—you name it. There are so many ways to keep from being stagnant and complacent.

Lastly, as I have previously mentioned, spend time with the Lord. He knows the plans that He has for you. He knows you better than you know yourself. Trust Him. He has sent His Holy Spirit to be with you and guide you into all truth.

This includes your mission and assignment. May the God of progress forever guide you all your days, and may success cover you in your endeavors.

PERSONAL GROWTH IS PERSONAL

PRAYER FOR YOUR PERSONAL GROWTH:

Father, thank You for choosing me. You could have selected anyone more qualified, but in Your mercy, You chose me. I ask that You would help me to develop my potential. I believe I am consecrated for a special work in this world. I believe You have assigned me to a specific purpose for a specific audience. I give You my life and everything I have. All is Yours.

In Jesus' name. Amen.

CHAPTER 9

DIE EMPTY

"Whatever your hand finds to do, do it with your might; for there is no work or device or knowledge or wisdom in the grave where you are going."
—Ecclesiastes 9:10 (NKJV)

WELL, YOU HAVE ARRIVED AT THE LAST CHAPTER of this book.

I pray that this is the chapter you come back to over and over. When you feel down. When you feel discouraged. When you feel like giving up. When you feel like you aren't enough.

Mark this page. Highlight it. Pray over it. I am going to do my best to put into writing what I have been carrying in my heart throughout this entire book. And, I thought it best to end it with this phrase: DIE EMPTY.

Yes, you read that correctly. Die empty.

It's a phrase I heard years ago from one of my favorite communicators—Dr. Myles Munroe. As a Christian, you will hear lots of messages over the course of your life if you attend church regularly and you are in the Word constantly. But, I think there are certain sermons and messages that impact you in such a way that it changes your walk, mind, and heart. You just aren't the same.

I want to give you an excerpt from his sermon that evening:

I saw the wealthiest spot on earth in your city today. I have concluded that the wealthiest spots on earth are not the oil fields of Iran, Iraq, or Saudi Arabia. The wealthiest spots on earth are not the diamond mines of South Africa. The wealthiest spots on earth are not the silver mines of Central America or the gold mines of South America. I discovered that the wealthiest spot on earth

PERSONAL GROWTH IS PERSONAL

is . . . actually not too far from your house. You have passed it and not even realized it. . . . The wealthiest spot on earth is the cemetery. The graveyard.

Because, in the cemetery, there are books that were never written.

The graveyard is filled with music that no one has ever heard.

The cemetery is filled with paintings that no one will ever see.

The graveyard is filled with poetry that no one will ever read.

The cemetery is filled with businesses that never opened.

The graveyard is filled with ideas that will never come to fruition.

It is filled with dreams that will never be a reality.

The graveyard is filled with great men who died as alcoholics.

The graveyard is filled with awesome women who died as drug addicts.

What a tragedy. If I could just mine the cemetery the way you mine for gold, I would be a rich man.

You have to make it a point to rob the grave.

What an image. What an illustration. This impacted me so much because I felt that I had so much more within me. As I mentioned at the beginning of this book, I knew my life was bigger than my body gave me credit for. I knew God had created me with much more potential than was being witnessed by the naked eye.

As you read that quote, did you think of you? Did you think of all the things God has called you to do and fulfill while you are alive? You have to make it a point to rob the grave.

Within you are things meant to stay here on earth. For within us are the following:

- Books
- Songs
- Ideas
- Businesses
- Ministries
- Buildings
- Fortunes
- Legacies

I wanted to write this segment to tell you to die—empty. Don't die old; die finished.

LEAVE NOTHING WITHIN ME

To die empty is a mindset that refuses to go to the grave without first delivering everything that has been deposited by Almighty God into your being. When my first child was born, I remember saying these words to my wife, "I wonder how God has already prepackaged her."

PERSONAL GROWTH IS PERSONAL

> **Don't die old; die finished.**

I said this because I had the revelation that she didn't come into this world empty. She came with gifts already within her. She came with purpose. As a parent, one of my desires is to help her discover her God-embedded purpose.

You also came with a code. Not just a genetic code, but a prophetic code. Like Jeremiah, you have been set apart for God's specific and divine plan. You may not be able to see it or feel it yet, but it's in you.

- There are things in YOU that are meant to set people free.
- There are things in YOU that are meant to give people a voice.
- There are things in YOU that will bless others.
- There are things in YOU that will be left behind, impacting others once you are long gone.

And, just because you leave this earth doesn't mean your message has to. Paul penned this well-known scripture hundreds of years ago as he was preparing to leave this world in 2 Timothy 4:6-8 (NKJV):

For I am already being poured out as a drink offering, and the time of my departure is at hand. I have fought the good fight, I have finished the race, I have kept the faith. Finally, there is laid up for me the crown of righteousness, which the Lord, the righteous Judge, will give to me on that Day, and not to me only but also to all who have loved His appearing.

This text is a deluge of power and hope. In the first century, it has been noted that Romans would end their meal with a cup of wine being poured out to their gods. Paul, a man of Christian faith, also knew that in his heritage of Judaism, a drink offering would also be poured out at the altar as a sacrifice before the Lord. In a way, Paul was saying the following, "The day is done, the meal is just about over, and I'm being poured out unto God." In other words, the liquid is completely emptied from the cup.

In the same manner, my heart's prayer is to leave empty. You can too.

ENEMIES OF DYING EMPTY

Are there obstacles that keep us from emptying ourselves completely? Yes. What holds us back from giving our all? There are many things, but I want to expose a few of them that I feel are more common and keep people from releasing what's within them.

Procrastination

This is defined as the action of delaying or postponing something. Years ago, a very famous preacher surveyed the Bible to find out what were the most important words in the Scripture. For instance, he wanted to find out what was the saddest word in the Bible and what was the happiest word. He listed all these words that had emotions attached to them. But when he came to the most dangerous word in the Bible, the word that he chose was "tomorrow."

Tomorrow can be a dangerous word, for tomorrow has robbed many dreamers of their dreams. I would say that tomorrow is the enemy's favorite word—while a word dear to the heart of the Father is today.

In Luke chapter 9:57-62, Jesus was speaking to some of his followers about discipleship, and he was trying to illustrate the importance of their immediate response to the call:

Now it happened as they journeyed on the road, that someone said to Him, "Lord, I will follow You wherever You go." And Jesus said to him, "Foxes have holes and birds of the air have nests, but the Son of Man has nowhere to lay His head." Then He said to another, "Follow Me." But he said, "Lord, let me first go and bury my father." Jesus said to him, "Let the dead bury their own dead, but you go and preach the kingdom of God." And another also said, "Lord, I will follow You, but let me first go and bid them farewell who are at my house." But Jesus said to him, "No one, having put his hand to the plow, and looking back, is fit for the kingdom of God."

A wise man once said, "Procrastination is the arrogant assumption that God will give you tomorrow what you were told to do today."

Neglect

The definition of neglect is to fail to care for properly. I am reminded of the parable of the talents in Matthew 25, where one servant was given five, another was given two, and the third one was given one. Each person was given talents according to their ability. Two of them did well with their talents and heard the words, "Well done, good and faithful servant; you were faithful over a few things. I will make you ruler over many things. Enter into the joy of your lord." But one of them didn't do anything with their talent. He just buried it. Kept it hidden. And his reception wasn't as great as the others who were fruitful, for he was told in Matthew 25:26-28 (NKJV):

"You wicked and lazy servant, you knew that I reap where I have not sown, and gather where I have not scattered seed. So you ought to have deposited my money with the bankers, and at my coming, I would have received back my own with interest. So take the talent from him, and give it to him who has ten talents."

To neglect means to ignore, to disregard, to be slack. Are there things you are ignoring that you know have been tugging at your heart? Paul tells Timothy in 1 Timothy 4:14 (NKJV), "Do not neglect the gift that is in you, which was given to you by prophecy with the laying on of the hands of the eldership."

Mindset

Go back and read the chapter on personal mindset. Many people never accomplish the will of God in their lives, not because the enemy was strong but because they just didn't think they could. Many times, we feel:

- Intimidated: We are afraid.
- Inferior: We are less than.
- Insecure: We aren't confident.

PERSONAL GROWTH IS PERSONAL

Most people focus on what they can't do rather than on what they can do. Did you know that your mind and body work together? Fear is physical, but so is courage. I would encourage you to make a note of what you can do. God has gifted you for such a time as this. You can make a difference. You can be used greatly. You can change.

A PROPHETIC WORD

As we come to the close of this book (I'm a preacher, so I'm used to closing a message), I want to end with a story. When I first started my preaching journey over two decades ago, a minister spoke over my life and said that the Lord was going to raise me up and use my voice to speak to nations. I remember this prophetic word so vividly as I received it with all of my heart. Fast forward to the present day, and the truth is I have only visited a few nations outside of my own. And, I haven't physically preached in other nations other than my own.

But . . . God.

I was asked to write some Bible school curriculum by a pastor beginning around 2011. He had wanted me to do teachings on effective youth ministry since I had the fruit in my own ministry. So, I gladly complied. It was such a great experience, and because his team and churches received it well, he went on to ask me to do several more sets of curriculum for these Bible schools he was planting all around the world through local churches. During that time, I felt I was supposed to do it, and it was a joy.

After the year of the pandemic of COVID-19, I reached out to him to see how he and his ministry were doing. I was just checking in since the Lord laid him on my heart. After an exchange of some words, he shared with me the following:

"Your four courses are currently being used in forty countries by twenty-two thousand students (mostly pastors and Christian workers), with five thousand current graduates. People are also listening to your teaching in numerous languages, including English, French, Spanish, Kirundi, Lingala, and Swahili. The courses are also blessing lives in fifteen refugee camps in numerous countries."

Mind blown.

I couldn't believe it. Right after I read that message, my eyes teared up, and I remembered the word of the Lord spoken over my life years ago. The Lord is truly faithful. But had I not stepped out in obedience, I would have never had that testimony.

What are you waiting for?

What's holding you back?

You don't have the right connections?

You don't have enough money, the right background or pedigree?

It doesn't matter. Do what the Lord is calling you to do. Fulfill your ministry and purpose. You have so much more inside of you, and others are waiting on your gift.

Paul died empty. Jesus died empty. He said, "It is finished." I repeat—don't die old; die finished. Die completely empty. Go to your grave as a drink offering completely poured out.

Say this out loud: "The world hasn't seen anything yet."

And go.

PERSONAL GROWTH IS PERSONAL

FINAL PRAYER FOR YOU:

Father, I thank You for the individual who has completed this book. I believe that it was for this time and season. Lord, I declare the words of Jabez in 1 Chronicles 4 over them at this moment in that You would bless them, indeed, and enlarge their territory, that Your hand would be with them, and that You would keep them from evil, that they may not cause pain.

Enlarge their growth.
Expand their minds.
Encourage their hearts.
Edify their spirits.

Use their life so that it would cause praise toward You.

We speak like Moses to our pharaohs, declaring freedom from bondage.

We prophesy like Ezekiel, commanding dry bones to live.

We strike the ground with our potential even as Elisha, commanding the king.

We release the proverbial stones toward our Goliath as David did.

We stand our ground like the mighty men refusing to give up territory.

We carry the promise in our wombs as Mary was instructed to do with Your Son.

We pursue the mission relentlessly as Paul in his missionary journeys.

And lastly, anoint their heads with oil, and may it overflow in every area of their life. Thank you for all that You will do, for Yours is the kingdom, and the power, and the glory—forever!

RESOURCES

Listed are books that helped me tremendously in my personal growth journey, and I hope will do the same for you:
1) *The 15 Invaluable Laws of Growth* by John Maxwell
2) *Necessary Endings* by Dr. Henry Cloud
3) *177 Mental Toughness Secrets of the World Class* by Steve Siebold
4) *Grit* by Angela Duckworth
5) *How to Lead When You're Not in Charge* by Clay Scroggins
6) *The One Thing* by Gary Keller and Jay Papasan
7) *As a Man Thinketh* by James Allen
8) *The Gift of Being Yourself* by David G. Benner
9) *The Talent Code* by Daniel Coyle
10) *Atomic Habits* by James Clear

Mentors (from afar) I have greatly benefitted from in certain areas of my life, and perhaps you could also:
1) John Maxwell—on leadership and communication
2) Craig Groeschel—on ministry
3) Myron Golden—on personal mindset

PERSONAL GROWTH IS PERSONAL

4) Patrick Leoncioni—on teams and working with people
5) Jordan Peterson—on general wisdom
6) Dr. Henry Cloud—on internal thought process
7) Dave Ramsey—on basic money management

Tests I have taken that gave me great insight about myself:
- DISC Test
- Strengths Finder Test from Strengthsfinder 2.0 by Tom Rath
- EQ Assessment from Emotional Intelligence 2.0 by Dr. Travis Bradberry and Dr. Jean Greaves
- The 6 Types of Working Geniuses by Patrick Lencioni
- A General Spiritual Gift Test Online (many are free)